PUNCH FEAR IN THE FACE
ESCAPE AVERAGE
DO WORK THAT MATTERS

# START.

## JON ACUFF

 LAMPO
PRESS
THE LAMPO GROUP, INC.

© 2013 Lampo Licensing, LLC
Published by Lampo Press, The Lampo Group, Inc.
Brentwood, Tennessee 37027

The opinions and conclusions expressed in this book are those of the author. All references to websites, blogs, authors, publications, brand names, and/or products are placed there by the author. No recommendation or endorsement by The Lampo Group, Inc., is intended, nor should any be implied. Some of the names of people mentioned have been changed to protect their privacy.

This publication is designed to provide accurate and authoritative information with regard to the subject matter covered. It is sold with the understanding that the publisher is not engaged in rendering financial, accounting, or other professional advice. If financial advice or other expert assistance is required, the services of a competent professional should be sought.

Editors: Brent Cole and Darcie Clemen
Cover design: Luke LeFevre and Melissa McKenney
Interior design: Thinkpen Design, Inc., www.thinkpendesign.com

ISBN: 978-1-937077-59-4

CIP Data application in process

"Dad, why is L.E.'s name mentioned three times in the dedication to *Quitter* and my name is mentioned only once?" —MCRAE, MY THEN 5-YEAR-OLD DAUGHTER

"Great question. You can write the dedication to the next book." —ME

"Good. I'll say, 'To Jenny, McRae, and L.E.'" —MCRAE

# CONTENTS

# 1

# YOU ARE HERE

**IF YOU EVER FLY KOREAN AIR,** keep your eyes closed as you make your way to coach. You may have to feel your way there, but trust me, that momentary inconvenience is worth it. You do not want to see the first-class seats.

The challenge is that you enter from the front of the plane. If your eyes are open, you're immediately thrust into an aeronautical wonderland. First class isn't full of seats; it's full of tiny pods of luxury. They have their own little sleeping cocoons in which to lounge away the sixteen-hour flight. And if you see these pleasure domes as you walk to your seat, you're going to get sad.

So that you fully comprehend what's happening as you pass through the seating classes, Korean Air color-codes the seats. The pleasure domes in first class are woven in a periwinkle blue fabric that seems to tickle you lightly and whisper, "Don't you wish this flight were longer?" The next class of seats is light blue, like the color of an apron you'd buy at Williams-Sonoma after being wooed into the store by the smell of boysenberry muffins. The business class is dark blue, serious but still seriously comfortable. Finally, at the end of the color wheel—and back of the plane—you get to coach class, your seat, which is brown, the color of disappointment.

The other thing it'd be good for you to know—should you ever find yourself flying to Asia—is that Vietnam is not close to South Korea. I thought they were like Connecticut and Rhode Island. That maybe I could look out the window from the airport in Seoul and see Vietnam across the water. I was wrong.

After flying sixteen hours from Atlanta to South Korea, we had to fly another six hours from Seoul to Hanoi. We then boarded an overnight train to travel deeper into the country. I don't know if there were periwinkle first-class seats available on that train, but I do know we didn't get them. The shared bathroom was just a metal hole in the floor that dropped straight onto the tracks. I thought it was kind of fun. My wife felt differently.

After a solid night of rumbling through moonlit mountains, we arrived in Sapa. From there we drove another seven hours on dirt roads overlooking cliffs. Imagine the most dangerous road you've ever been on, remove all the guardrails, and then add water buffalo.

Finally, after hours of breathtaking scenery punctuated by moments of sheer panic, we came upon something I'd never expected to see. French motorcyclists.

My initial confusion was that they weren't on skinny ten-speeds from the 1960s with long sticks of crusty French bread sticking out of wicker baskets, and none of them were wearing jaunty berets. (Everything I know about France I learned from puzzles. And it's completely okay for me to poke fun at France. The only language my books have ever been translated into is German. I'm like Hasselhoff over there.)

Decked out in apocalyptic-looking safety gear and a week's worth of dirt, they were obviously a long way from home. Lost in the deepest middle of nowhere I'd ever experienced, the bikers were gesturing to some Vietnamese villagers huddled around a map that was unfolded on the handlebars of one of the bikes.

We pulled over to the side of the road to help them find their next destination. Steve, an American who had lived in Asia for eighteen years, looked out the bus window at the bikers' map.

"Wow," he said to Hua, our Vietnamese driver, "that is an amazing map. Look how detailed it is! We should get one of those."

Then he paused just before lowering his window and said, "Then again, the best map in the world doesn't matter if you don't know where you are."

* * *

Steve was right. Without a point of origin, even the best map is rendered useless. If you opened up the GPS on your phone right now and tried to get directions, the very first thing the phone would need to know is where you are. Google Earth can't give you directions across the state or even across the street without a point of origin. Yet most of us, when it comes to figuring out where we're headed in life, never stop to ask the simple question, "Where am I?"

We just keep marching forward, day after day, cubicle after cubicle, moving faster and faster but not really going anywhere. Eventually, at the end of our lives, we start to do some questioning. We finally pause long enough to reexamine our decisions and maybe even ask hard questions of young, single-browed authors on airplanes.

That's what a grandmother in her early 70s did to me on a flight from Dallas to Baltimore. She was flying back from a gambling trip in Reno with her sister. They were two grandmothers on the run, laughing and joking with each other in the back of a Southwest plane. During the flight, I gave her a copy of my book *Quitter*. I promise, I don't do that every time I fly. I don't wear cargo pants full of my books and then say, "Oh, what's this? How did this get in my pocket? That's crazy! It's my *Wall Street Journal* best-selling book! I'll sign it for you, but please, no flash photography. It dries out my pores."

But we had been talking about life and dreams, and giving her a copy of *Quitter*, which addresses both, seemed like an okay thing to do.

After she had been reading it for an hour, she leaned in to speak over the engine noise and ask me a question I wasn't ready for.

"What do you do when all the excuses you used to not chase your dream are gone? What do you do then?"

There was sadness in her words. A sense of fear and resignation that seemed to suck all the joy out of a boisterous weekend trip with a sister. Sadder still, I didn't have an answer for her. I didn't know the answer, but I knew there was one.

There had to be, because I didn't want you or me to get to 80 or 90 years old and realize we mortgaged the best years of our lives doing something we weren't called to do. I didn't want to look back on life and wonder where it all went.

That happened to me once when I was 30. Through a series of bad decisions, I finally woke up one day in a cubicle and realized I'd coasted through the last ten years of my life. And I knew that same thing would happen again if I wasn't careful.

Realizing where I was headed, I started to write about that woman's question. I wrote 50,000 words trying to find the answer, but like most things in life, it snuck up on me when I was looking the other way.

One afternoon while meeting with a friend, I started to dissect Dave Ramsey's life on a whiteboard. He's been an incredibly successful author and businessman, something I aspire to be too. I was curious how he accomplished so much. As I started to map out the trajectory of his life, I made a pretty simple discovery about what it takes to be awesome. It's not that complicated or unique; in fact, since the dawn of time, every awesome life has gone through the same five stages.

## 1. Learning
## 2. Editing
## 3. Mastering
## 4. Harvesting
## 5. Guiding

Like a simple map through life, those are the five stages on the road to awesome. And until recently, they have matched up pretty closely with your age.

### In your 20s, you resided in Learning.

You went to college, got a job, or joined the military. You didn't yet know what you were made of, so you sampled many endeavors and did as much as you could to learn about yourself, the world around you, and where you best fit in.

### In your 30s, you moved on up to Editing.

You started to focus on the handful of things that worked well in your 20s. You were not done learning, but you started editing down the list of things you thought were really important. You prioritized your passions. You eliminated old habits that wrecked you in your 20s and concentrated on doing more of the things you love and less of the things you hate. It was a winnowing period. You focused your career, your relationships, and every part of your life.

### In your 40s, you ascended to Mastering.

You edited your life to the most important things in your 30s, and then it came time to master them. You were going to be an awesome parent, awesome friend, awesome employee, etc. You didn't narrow your life further; you just had greater certainty about what you were good at and how to do it regularly. You were no longer the young upstart at work; you were the one with fifteen to twenty years of experience. Tried and true. You started leading bigger projects and initiatives. You were not an expert yet, but you were next in line.

### In your 50s, you basked in Harvesting.

The seeds you planted in your 20s, 30s, and 40s finally began blooming. You made the most money in your career during this decade and reaped what you sowed. This wasn't rocket science. If you spent your 30s and 40s working hard to be considered an expert in your field, you would obviously have more job opportunities than if you jumped around forty-seven times and blamed your bosses for "not recognizing your talent." If you were deliberate about pouring into relationships in your 20s, 30s, and 40s, guess what? You harvested abundant relationships in your 50s. When your collegiate son crashed his car, you harvested an outpouring of support and love. Lots of people came to the hospital, and someone probably even brought a casserole.

## In your 60s, you entered a place of Guiding.

You retired with a gold watch and a ranch-style home in Florida. You were a grandfather or a grandmother. You were the elder statesman, the one with the wisdom. You got to give back generously to people who were traveling the path on which you spent forty-plus years. Corncob pipe whittling was not mandatory but highly likely.

If you wanted to achieve awesomeness, that's the path you followed. Tens of thousands of people have proved it's the way to awesome.

If it's that easy to walk down the path though, if the steps are so clearly marked, why don't more people do it? Well, the bad news is it's not the only path on the map. And, like a back road through the mountains, the path to awesome is much narrower than the other, more common path.

Billions of people have traveled and continue to travel the other path, and it grows wider every year. The terrain is easy—grassy even—and after a brief incline it follows a safe and steady decline that mostly allows for casual coasting.

It sounds nice. It feels effortless when you're on it.

The trouble is that on this wide path, you don't end up at awesome. You just end up at old. This path is called "average."

The trickiest thing is that both paths begin in the same place. And both paths end in harvesting and guiding.

The key difference is that if you've trekked the path of awesome, the harvest is abundant and you will guide other people down their own abundant paths. If, on the other hand, you've coasted the path of average, never daring to believe you could learn, edit, and master your own bit of awesomeness, you will harvest a crop neither you nor anyone else desires. And you will then guide, but instead of illuminating an awesome path for others, you'll become a lighthouse indicating the rocks on which you crashed your life.

You may not have a haunted house or an abnormally large furnace in the basement à la *The Burbs*, but people will still refer to you in hushed tones like they did my old neighbors.

They grew so bitter that they eventually decided to spend their time making sure any ball or Frisbee that lighted upon their lawn was quickly confiscated and cataloged. After a few years of draining the entire neighborhood of toys, they took my friend Marc to court, at which point they presented all their evidence. I can only imagine the jury's faces as they were presented with Wiffle balls bearing dates on them.

Is that what you want your life to come to? Wiffle ball CSI? Me neither.

So then why do most people decide to travel down the average path?

The truth is they don't decide. The only thing you have to do on the average path is not die.

You graduate from high school or college and effectively shift into neutral. Sure, you're not moving that fast, but you're getting great gas mileage and you are making some progress, if you want to call it that. You're definitely getting older and that means something, right? With age comes wisdom? Not necessarily.

Especially if you're coasting. Eventually, you'll roll your way right into the grave.

The average path is the easier of the two paths, and it's dangerously comfortable. I spent many years on it without realizing I'd been there a week.

The awesome path?

It is dangerous too—but the good kind of dangerous. The kind of dangerous through which all great accomplishments must travel. On it are tall mountains, rocky walls, and even an occasional dragon. You're going to get bloodied, your discipline will be tested, and your dreams will be challenged a thousand times over. But ohhhh, it is awesome.

And here's the kicker: when I say it's awesome, I don't mean "eventually" awesome. I'm talking right-this-second awesome.

I'd never write a book that said, "In forty years you'll get to harvest some amazing stuff in your life if you'll just suck it up for four decades." I don't want a life like that. Why would I convince you that you needed one?

## AWESOME IS AVAILABLE LIKE NEVER BEFORE

The opportunity and speed with which you can reach awesome has never been greater. Three forces of nature have collided to create a once-in-a-century storm even bigger than the one Patrick Swayze surfed at the end of *Point Break*. (Google it.)

## 1. Retirement is dead.

My friend Luke's mom was a teacher at the same school for twenty-eight years. She was going to retire eventually because that's what you did. You worked in one place, trusted in Social

Security, and then retired comfortably in a house that had accrued value over a few decades. Then she got laid off. Suddenly, like millions of people in their 40s and 50s, she found herself facing the daunting task of starting a new career or what people are labeling an "encore career." In her mid-50s, she had to be 20 again. She's not alone. In 2011, 20 percent of new entrepreneurs were between the ages of 55 and 64.[1]

While the market will recover, the ideals won't. The government, the company, the house—you can't rely on them for warmth when you tuck into your 60s for a long winter's nap. In addition, some experts believe the retirement age will eventually stretch to 70 or 80.[2] That's decades longer than the finish line my wife's grandfather crossed. For a generation in their 50s, that means starting over. For a generation in their 30s and 40s, that means aiming for a completely different finish line. Retirement is dead.

## 2. Hope is boss.

Do you know how many people in my college graduating class of 1998 launched projects to build wells in Africa? Do you know how many asked what percentage of their hoodie purchase was going to Haiti? Do you know how many wore TOMS shoes? The answer in each case is zero. Changing the world was something you cared about eventually, not right away, and brilliant books reflected that. In *Halftime*, Bob Buford told Boomers that after spending the first half of their lives focused on success, it was time to spend the second half focused on significance and changing the world. If you told a 22-year-old today that before he can change the world he has to work for twenty years, he'd giggle at you. Generation Y, and Generation X as they are inspired by the shift in culture, want meaning now, not eventually. Hope is boss.

### 3. Anyone can play.

In 2000, I paid a designer $2,000 to build me a website. He charged by the page and learned how to develop it by reading a book. A book! Isn't that adorable? We thought the dawn of the Internet removed all the gatekeepers. It didn't. It just introduced new gatekeepers. Like developers and designers and social media experts. Those days are waning, though. Moms are making millions on blogs. Teenagers are starting businesses on Facebook. People are building empires on Pinterest. Specialists still exist, but technology is finally available to the entire population. Anyone can play.

I'm not a futurist. I'm a presentist, which isn't even a real word but sounds less lame than "right nowist." Those three forces I just described aren't on the horizon. They are the horizon—for you and me and anyone who is willing to escape average.

As a result, you can be more awesome, more often, a whole lot faster today.

The Internet revolution isn't over. It's barely started. And one of the biggest things it's done is radically shorten the path to reaching your dreams.

While the fives stages of awesome have held true for decades, reaching awesome used to be primarily a post-midlife accomplishment. You had to gain experience plus earn money or pedigree or degrees from institutions where they wear ascots and play, not just eat, squash. The path to awesome was decades long and there was little you could do to shorten it. Everyone had to put in his or her time.

The Internet, and especially social media, has changed that. You just have to find your starting point and stay on the right path.

In 2008, I started a blog in my kitchen. I didn't have a fancy design. I didn't have any photos. I didn't have any sort of tech-savvy skills that made me a perfect candidate for social media. I used the free template that Blogspot offered, and I didn't even start with an original idea. There was another blog called *Stuff White People Like*. It was a satire of Caucasia. I thought it would be funny to create a Christian version of that site. So I did, with the expectation that I'd get bored of it in a week or two and move on. After all, the other fifty horrible URLs I had registered at GoDaddy.com didn't sustain a whole lot of momentum. "Word-Ninja.com" went nowhere.

I told 100 friends about the site and started writing goofy paragraphs. On the eighth day of its existence, 4,000 people from around the world showed up to read it. Turns out the 100 friends had passed the URL to 100 friends who had passed the URL to 100 friends who eventually told people in Singapore to read it.

Can you even begin to fathom how I would have shared my ideas with 4,000 people in eight days for free thirty years ago? What would I have done, a door-to-door marketing campaign? Me just knocking on people's front doors and saying, "Hi, I have some ideas about how it's weird that some people front hug you and other people side hug you. It's kind of this 'I like you enough to give you one arm of appreciation but let's not get all crazy and embrace with both arms.' Can I please come sit in your living room and read you some of my other ideas? When we're done, do you mind calling your friends on your rotary phone, which is bolted to your kitchen wall, to let them know I am available for home readings of my ideas? Also, do you know anyone in other countries, like Singapore for instance? Do you mind giving them a ring too? Thanks!"

That would have never worked. And if that were my only path to awesome, I'd still be on the average path. A few years ago, you and I had only a few chances to find our path to an awesome life. Ultimately, you just hoped you picked the right track when you were young and got a big break along the way.

It's not that we all chose average. No one aims for that in the beginning. Nobody says, "I'm going to be average for sixty-five years and then die!" But not long ago, the path to awesome was so long and arduous that most of us chose not to start. That, or we tried, and failed, to find a shortcut.

I looked at life that way, too, until 2008.

That's the year I discovered the path to awesome had changed. Namely, it was something that could be traveled much more quickly, before eyelid wrinkles started to appear. I started by taking small steps—steps that I eventually learned social media could greatly accelerate.

After my blog started to grow a little, I thought it might make for an interesting book. Having spent a decade on the average path, I tried a very average way to get it published. I asked a friend who worked at a big church if he knew anyone at any of the major publishers. He had a friend who had a friend at one of the largest publishers on the planet. He told her about my book idea and asked if she would pass the idea to the publisher. She did, and this is her verbatim response:

*I actually mentioned this to the publisher this morning on a call I had with them, and to be honest, they feel pretty full up right now. Their recommendation would be to continue to see how the blog readership goes and perhaps explore connecting with a smaller, boutique publishing house that could give him the attention he wants and deserves if this is indeed his calling.*

*Not what you want to hear, but that is what they suggested at this time.*

That's fancy talk for "no."

That's where the average path got me, and it makes sense. Who did I think I was to write a book? I'd never written a book before. I'd never spoken publically before. I'd never done anything in my entire life that would make me attractive to a publisher.

If I stayed on the average path, the steps I'd take to get a book published were pretty clear. I'd spend my 30s slowly building a name for myself. I'd start going to writers' conferences. I'd buy a big thick book with publishers' addresses in it and mail off my manuscript a thousand times. I'd join a writers' circle and maybe figure out a way to self-publish a few of my ideas and call them scholarly articles. In my 40s, I'd keep plugging away at my manuscript, count my rejection letters, grow a frustrated writer's beard, and hope that in my 50s I had paid enough dues to get a book published. In my 60s, I'd then get to sit my grandkids on my knee, set aside my corncob pipe, and tell them an epic forty-year yarn called, "How Grandpa Finally Got His Book Published." It would teach them perseverance, theoretically.

Ugh.

That's the average path. Depressing, right?

Fortunately for you and me, we're growing up in the middle of a revolution. (I use that word sparingly. Whenever another author tells me, "This isn't a book; this is a revolution!" I know it's just a book.)

Social media gave me a chance to build a platform. For free. The only costs were time and hustle. Social media gave me access to an audience. It gave me a public arena to hone my writing skills with instant, international feedback.

Social media offered me an opportunity to become a legitimate author much sooner than 50 years old. I accepted the challenge and jumped in with both feet.

A few months later, my agent and I submitted my book proposal back to publishers. Only this time I included information about my blog audience. Number of readers, number of comments, number of fans in numbers of countries. That completely changed the conversation.

I was no longer invisible. I was no longer a nobody with an idea. I was a writer with proven skills as evidenced by a quantifiable readership. As a result, two publishers bid for the book. Guess who won? Guess who published my first book?

The same publisher who initially rejected it via my friend.

My story isn't that unique or that impressive. Pebble Technology, the company that created a customizable wristwatch that few had ever heard of, raised $10.2 million from more than 68,000 supporters on www.kickstarter.com.[3] They raised their first million in twenty-eight hours. Can you imagine how long it would have taken to find 68,000 donors without the tools of the Internet?

Clearly there are now ways to accelerate your life down the path to awesome, even if you never use social media. (If you decide to use social media, though, I put my top ten tips on page 239.)

Once you know how the map works, you can shorten the time you spend in each destination. You can game the map. You don't have to wait until you are 50 to harvest. You don't have to wait until you are 40 to be an expert. And you don't have to be 20 to start a new adventure.

## WE ALL USED TO BE AWESOME

Awesome is a lot simpler than you think, because you used to know awesome quite well.

Everyone did at one point. Especially when we were kids.

I was reminded of this one night as I was walking down the hall at home. My daughters were brushing their teeth, an event that usually boils over to an international crisis. This time, though, they weren't fighting for sink space—they were talking literature.

I heard L.E., my 9-year-old, say to her little sister, McRae, "Did you know that the guy who wrote *The Twits* also wrote *James and the Giant Peach*?"

I heard McRae respond, "I know! I love that guy. He's got a great imagination, like me."

*Like me.*

What a powerful declaration.

Roald Dahl has been called the greatest storyteller of our generation. He also wrote *Charlie and the Chocolate Factory*. He's sold millions and millions of books. And in McRae's little 6-year-old mind, his imagination is on par with hers. He's her peer.

You used to believe like that too. You used to turn sticks into swords or dirty flip-flops into glass slippers. You climbed trees and made forts and thought being a doctor wasn't out of reach. Nothing was out of reach.

Then, somewhere along the way, you lost it.

Maybe someone who mattered to you told you that your version of awesome didn't matter. When my friend Liz was in the eighth grade, she loved to dance. It was all she ever did. One day, her mom pulled her aside and said, "You know you're not going to be a Rockette, right? You know that's not in the cards for you, right?"

Do you think Liz danced a whole lot after that? Of course not. She gave up her dream of awesome that day.

As a parent, I understand the temptation to tell your kid something like that. You don't want Simon Cowell to be the first person who introduces your daughter to the idea that she can't sing. But there's an inherent problem with this approach to life. When a parent, a boss, a teacher, a spouse, or a friend tells you what you *can't* be, they're predicting a future they don't control. They don't know what 25 or 35 or 55 looks like for you.

What if, when he didn't make the varsity basketball team his sophomore year of high school, Michael Jordan's dad had pulled him aside and, putting his arm around a young Michael, said, "You know you're not going to play in the NBA, right? You know that's not in the cards for you, don't you?"

Maybe your mom never told you that your dream was too big, but chances are you've been telling yourself that for years—maybe decades. The way your brain developed certainly hasn't helped the cause.

When you were young, your right hemisphere or "right brain" was in full force. It was the guy in charge, and it was the part of your brain that embraced curiosity and adventure and was constantly unafraid to ask *Why?* and *Why not?* Your brain was this way when you were a child because you were learning at a rapid clip. You were learning language and the laws of physics and the elements of balance. You had to be unguarded so you could absorb everything—even some pain here and there—so you would know how to thrive in this land called life-outside-the-womb.

But as you grew older, the other hemisphere, the "left brain" began to gain a voice. It began to say things like, "That's impossible," or, "They will laugh at you," or, "Don't be foolish." Your left brain plays an important role in your thinking because it is the voice that teaches you to not touch the hot stove or jump off the top stair like you are a superhero. Unfortunately, it can also make a very logical and compelling argument that what it says is final. As we grew up, most of us came to believe the left brain's assertions, and as a result we lost the sense that awesome was around the corner. Instead, we started to believe that awesome was not in the cards for us or that it was illogical or simply "childish."

The good news is we can recover those childlike notions of grandeur. But it takes more than simply acting like a child again. You know some things as an adult that you couldn't have known as a child. And you possess some skills that no child can develop. While I encourage you to think like my daughter does about the famous author—because your perception does truly fuel your reality—the best news is that now you can apply that thinking like an adult. The road to awesome is still accessible. Now, as an adult, you have the tools to head down it immediately.

We've been told our whole lives that our 20s are when we begin down our career paths. And our 60s are the end of the road.

But that timeline is no longer the only valid one. In fact, that timeline is no longer typical.

Age is no longer the primary factor that determines where you are on the map. Life is now less about how old you are and more about when you decide to live.

If you're 45 and looking for a career shift after realizing you don't love what you do, you're back in your 20s. It's time to start.

If you're 33 and haven't found something you're really passionate about, you're still in your 20s. It's time to start.

If you're 52 and embarking on a new career because your job (and maybe your entire industry) disappeared, you've returned to your 20s. It's time to start.

If you're 22, well that one seems really obvious, doesn't it? You're literally in your 20s. It's time to start.

Regardless of your age or station in life, it all comes down to one simple truth: you just have to start.

# THE START

**IN CHAPTER 3, WE'LL PIÑATA FEAR,** but for now, please know this—it's schizophrenic.

Fear tends to argue both sides of the coin, leaving you absolutely no room to stand. Here are two of the complete opposite things it will tell you: "Don't chase your dream at all." And, "If you chase your dream, you have to do it all at once."

Do you see the absurdity of that? "Don't do it! Don't do it! Don't do it!" fear screams. Then, when you ignore those cries, fear changes its tactic and screams, "Do it all at once! Do it all at once!"

Both of those statements are lies.

As you stand with one foot still on the road to average and one foot on the road to awesome, you've got to kill those concerns. Fortunately, there's a trick that will take care of them both.

Just start.

It's going to be a tiny start. A small start. A move the size of the frozen yogurt sample cups they give you, even though they know you're secretly gaming the system and trying to eat your body weight in tiny portions of Cable Car Chocolate before they catch on.

You're just going to be a Starter.

The starting line is the only line you completely control.

The start is the only moment you're the boss of.

The finish? Don't kid yourself. That's months, if not years, away. You are going to meet dozens of people who are going to impact your finish. You are going to have countless opportunities, experiences, and challenges that dot the map of awesome you're following. There are cliffs and rivers and jungles you can't begin to fathom. You are going to stand on a mountaintop that is better than anything you ever dreamed and laugh at the idea that you thought you could plot out your finish.

The start? You own that, son. That's yours.

Every industry on the planet is littered with examples of this truth. Take the Segway, for instance. Do you remember those? That device was supposed to change the way we walked. One expert said, "If enough people see the machine, you won't have to convince them to architect cities around it. It'll just happen."

That quote is crazy because the expert didn't say, "Builders will construct houses around it." They said people will "architect cities around it." Whole cities will be impacted by this machine. Not homes. Not streets. *Entire cities.* Who made that outlandish claim? A guy named Steve Jobs. If anyone should be able to predict finish lines it's him, but he couldn't.[1]

The same is true in publishing. Kathryn Stockett's best-selling book, *The Help*, was rejected sixty times before it got published. Sixty different people said, "This book will never finish well."[2]

They were all wrong.

So was my friend Tim. (Name changed because I'm about to embarrass him.)

He's an author, and he endorses every book that's sent his way. He's probably endorsed forty different books in the last two years. He never said no. Finally he found one that he thought was a little too cheesy. He didn't want his name on the back cover of that one. So he passed. He turned down one endorsement in 2011. Want to know the name of the book?

*Heaven Is for Real.*

It sold more than ten million copies. Sony picked it up to turn into a movie.

He could have had his name advertised to ten million readers who like books similar to the kind he writes. But he didn't see that finish.

And neither will you.

It's impossible to accurately predict the finish. Part of the reason it's so difficult is that the path often radically changes by the time we get to the end. That's certainly been the case in my own life.

## I'M ON THE NEWS

It was midnight and I was pacing nervously in a New York hotel trying to memorize five names. They were given to me over the phone two hours earlier and if I messed them up in the morning, millions of people would know.

"Don't go viral for the wrong reasons," my wife said to me as I left Nashville that morning.

That was my fear—that in five hours when I was on the national news station, I'd throw up in my sleeve or fall over or be so sweaty with anxiety that I'd slide right off the couch. The host would watch me glide down to the floor and be forced to cover my unexpected exit by saying, "I thought Gary Busey was a squirrely interview, but Jon Acuff . . ."

And then there were those five names, the names of companies the producer wanted me to talk about. I was going on the show to talk about five companies that were hiring right then. The only problem was that I'd never heard of the companies.

Fast-forward a few hours, and I was sitting on a couch in makeup with four Kia-sized cameras pointed at me. The hosts were sitting next to me, prettier and handsomer than you can possibly imagine. One of the guys looked like a more attractive Ryan Reynolds. The woman next to me, who was probably a supermodel in her off time, asked me my question: "What companies are hiring right now?"

I rattled off the five names. I stuck it like an Olympic gymnast. Boom! Worst part is over. Then she asked her next question.

"What types of jobs are they hiring for?"

*Wait—what? What types of jobs? I don't know. I didn't know these companies existed until seven hours ago.*

Unfortunately, when you're on the news and you're an expert at helping people find their dream job, you can't say, "No clue. Good ones, I hope. Is it hot in here? Everyone sure is pretty."

So like a deer caught in high-definition headlights, I blinked a few times and threw out the only thing I could think of: "All types. From entry level to executive."

Yes! Covered the whole range at once. That's got to be true, right? At least one of those companies is hiring a janitor, and at least one is hiring someone who wears pleated pants and has a car with a mahogany steering wheel. I was out of the woods, or so I thought. Then the newscaster asked me another question:

"If I don't live in one of the states that these companies are located in, how do I find out about these jobs?"

*Seriously? You are killing me, lady! How do I know? I don't even know what states these companies are in. Did we go to college together? Is that what this is about? I was a jerk to you in college, and like a bad ABC drama, you've slowly planned revenge against me these last fourteen years? Now your plan has finally come to fruition. I'm wearing makeup (something no one tells you that you'll have to do when you write a book) on national television, and you're throwing haymakers at me.*

*All right, let's do this then.*

"Well, the best way to find out information about the jobs that are available is via the company's corporate website. That's going to be your best bet."

And I was out. I was feeling okay about that answer. It wasn't the greatest; I essentially said, "Google. You're going to want to Google it up, ma'am."

Then, as I walked off the set, had the makeup artist remove the layer of base from my face, and stepped into a limousine for the ride back to LaGuardia, I thought to myself, *This is exactly how I thought things would go when I started my blog.*

Sitting there in my kitchen, writing that first 200-word post, I knew that four years later I'd be sitting on a couch talking with millions of people. I knew I'd go from doing zero public-speaking gigs in 2007 to speaking to 80,000 people in 2011. I knew I'd write four books and eventually be forced to shave my unibrow into two distinct eyebrows because the camera hates a man with a single brow.

It happened just as exactly as I planned.

Only it didn't.

Filing paperwork in a cubicle for ten years didn't give me any indication of the changes that would occur once I started. The finish was unclear. I had no idea where it would all lead. And I'm so glad, because the truth is, the surprises life gives are always better than the things you think you see coming.

Publishing a book was a surprise to me. Moving to Nashville to work for Dave Ramsey was a surprise to me. Building two kindergartens in Vietnam was a surprise to me. And if I told you those were things I carefully planned along my career path, I would be a liar. The best things that have happened to me in the last five years weren't things I planned.

But I was the one who took that first step across the starting line. The one who said, "Let's see where this goes!"

That's the tension you'll have to face. You have to work incredibly hard on your start. You have to be deliberate and intentional and focused. You have to be a Starter. And then you have to be brave enough and prepared enough to react when a surprise presents itself.

When Dave asked me to think about joining his team, he didn't call me out of the blue. I'd spoken to his entire team three times already. I'd spent two years interacting with his company. I'd been on the road booking my own speaking gigs, writing my first book, and learning as much as I could on my own. I'd been starting.

When he offered me a job and a path diverged before me, I was ready. I'd spent two years starting, and I was ready to run once the next leg of the journey came into view.

## DON'T PLAN YOUR LIFE LIKE I USED TO PLAN MY SPEECHES

One afternoon in Atlanta, a guy named Lanny gave me some horrible feedback. I'd spoken at two camps he'd put on for about 5,000 students, and he had some evaluations he needed to go over with me.

The feedback was horrible because it was true.

According to Lanny, ten to fifteen people who saw me speak said that I "lacked passion" for my material. He said they felt like it was a performance, not material I was really passionate about.

I sat there a little stunned at first. I like to get feedback that says, "You're awesome. Almost too awesome. You don't need spotlights on you when you speak because the glow of your greatness illuminates the stage." And this feedback was not that.

The crowd thought I was fake. They thought I was going through the motions. They thought I was performing words I'd memorized.

And the sad thing is, they were right.

At the time, I was practicing my speeches eight to ten times per gig. I'd stand in my office, face out the window toward the Cracker Barrel next door, and do a full dry run of each speech. Over and over I would practice until I knew every line of my forty-five-minute speech.

I'd do all the hand motions, time myself, and even give pauses for the invisible crowd to laugh in my office. (Invisible people think I'm hilarious!)

I practiced this way because I didn't want to feel out of control onstage. I was so worried about making a mistake that I tightly clutched my hands around my speech. I had it perfectly mani-cured so I could control every second. No surprises.

Lanny picked up on that and gave me some advice: "Jon, your speeches are so over-structured that you're not leaving any space in them for something new to happen in the moment. That's the best part of a speech, when something brand new appears. When there's a surprise that both the audience and the speaker get to share. That's what connects an audience with a speaker, the feeling that you're going on a journey together, creating something together, and neither one of you knows exactly where it's going to go, but you'll end up there together."

Giving a speech that way takes a courage I didn't have at the time, and so does taking your first step on the road to awesome.

Average is so popular because average is familiar. We all know how to do average. Ninety-nine percent of the people on the planet do average. The road is well worn, the decisions are obvious, and the next steps are crystal clear.

Awesome? It's a little dangerous. There may be dragons in those woods (spoiler alert: there are). There are foggy mornings and cloudy nights. Sometimes you're not completely sure about your next step until you take it.

Average is predictable. Awesome is adventurous. So when faced with the decision to be awesome or stay average, most of us opt for the familiar, for the comfortable. Oh, we like the idea of an awesome adventure, but most of us default to trying to manicure the road to awesome so it's as safe and predictable as the road to average.

We want to plan the road to awesome. We want to talk about our ten-year visions. We want to detail every step before we take a single one. To make sure there's no room for

mistakes or failure. But when we do that, when we squeeze our lives and purposes that tightly, we eliminate any room for surprises.

We don't have time for them. They don't fit within our plan. They don't have any runway in our day to land on. We scowl when people interrupt what we're doing at work, grumble when neighbors want to talk at the mailbox, and curse momentary distractions to a day we've planned.

The road to awesome, though, is defined by the surprises. It's not a block in a downtown city laid out long ago by methodical city planners. It's a rambling dirt road with twists and turns that offers something new at every corner. Let's leave room on our maps for some surprises.

## THIS IDEA COST ME $2,310—PLEASE READ IT CAREFULLY

If taking the first step on the road to awesome were easy, then everybody would already be on it. The road to average would be empty, with just average-sized tumbleweeds blowing along at average speeds on average-temperature days.

The first step isn't easy, though, and one of the hard things is that you have to get comfortable with tension. You have to step into tension. You have to be:

**a realist and a dreamer
practical and impractical
logical and illogical**

You have to be brutally realistic about your present circumstances and wildly unrealistic about your future circumstances.

If you don't embrace this tension, if you don't accept it and make it work to your favor, you'll end up stealing money from your grandmother's church.

That's what happened to me.

Six years ago, I was feeling restless at my job. If you read *Quitter*, this is not surprising to you. I had made a backward career move—because I wrecked my job at Home Depot—and ended up working at After Hours. Though at first blush that sounds like a ladies dance establishment, I assure you it was not, though given my green belt in Kenpo I could probably be a bouncer if I had the time.

After Hours was actually a formalwear company that specialized in rental tuxedos. If you're playing along at home, I went from being one of the copy chiefs at a multibillion-dollar national brand to writing product copy trying to convince teenagers to rent my pants for the prom. Like a boss.

During my less-than-lustrous career at After Hours, I decided to start an ad agency. I'd worked at a small agency before and thought, *How hard can it be?* So I started one with a guy I knew from church. We got a whole bunch of business cards printed with our logo that kind of looked like the ThunderCats, registered our business, and went looking for a client.

We had huge aspirations. We were going to be a massive agency with hundreds of clients, a dream mirrored by our need to order thousands of business cards. Next step? Get someone to pay us to do whatever it is we thought we were capable of doing.

Our first client was a church in Charlotte, North Carolina. My dad's a pastor, so I understood the mechanics of that world. We were able to convince an incredibly kind woman at the church that our new company could build them a top-notch website. We put together an impressive proposal, and we agreed to build the site for around $30,000.

The church, showing wisdom, didn't pay us the entire amount up-front and only gave us an initial payment of about $12,000.

Then we got to work. I built a crazy site map, trying to make sense of the thousands of disconnected web pages this church had. The youth department had built their own site; the senior adults had their own section; everyone who had access to a computer had seemingly added a page to this tangled mess. I did my best to make sense of it and then turned over the project to my partner.

That last paragraph makes me sound like a good guy.

The truth is, I bailed on the project. I walked away and left him completely in the lurch. It was a train wreck, and I thought that maybe my partner could magically make sense of it.

Months into the project, a few realities about my present circumstances started to catch up with me: I didn't know how to run a business. I had never built a website before. Neither my partner nor I had any web developing skills.

After many sweaty nights, we decided to pull the plug and refund the church their remaining money. (Some had been spent on a third-party design firm we had hired to fix reality number 3.)

In the meantime, my partner moved with his family to another state, and I waited patiently for the whole situation to fade into the sunset of my life. But like a zombie who continues to crawl after you without legs, that thing was not going away easily.

The church had not received their refund check. My partner had sole control of the money. I called him over and over again and didn't get a response. I started to hate his voicemail greeting, which played John Mayer's song "Waiting on the World to Change." I wanted to punch John Mayer in the face.

Finally I got through to him and he agreed to overnight the money.

Two days later, I got a voicemail while at my day job: "Hi Jon, this is Sara! Hope you're having a good day. The check you sent us bounced. Please give me a call back."

Cue vomit.

The check we had sent—to the church my grandmother had attended for thirty years—bounced.

The money was gone. The account was empty. My partner had spent it.

How had this happened? It's painfully simple. I broke my own rule: I wasn't brutally realistic about my present and was wildly unrealistic about my future.

I got the second part right. I crushed that part! I had big, crazy, unrealistic dreams about my future circumstances. (Please refer to my note about the number of business cards we ordered, most of which are still in my garage. One day, when I'm really, really huge, I'll sell them on eBay for millions!)

Where I failed, and where you will too if you're not careful, is that I was wildly unrealistic about my future *and* my present.

That was my biggest mistake. Had I been brutally realistic about my present circumstances, I would have realized:

1. I didn't know the guy from church that well. We'd only known each other for six months. We didn't have enough relationship equity to justify me trusting him with sole control of all the money for our ad agency.

2. I didn't have much time to dedicate to the agency. I had a full-time job, a family, and a lot of other responsibilities I'd already committed to.
3. I didn't have any of the aforementioned skills needed to make this project successful.

Had I accepted all that and been honest about my present, that doesn't mean I wouldn't have started the agency. Not at all. That's the great misconception—that if you're honest about your present you can't be hopeful about your future. That realism has no role in dreaming.

Realism wouldn't have prevented me from chasing my dream; it would have prevented me from chasing the wrong dream. I would have done a different project. I would have said to the church, "We're new; can we do a beta project for you? Something small like creating a new site for your preschool department? If that goes well, we can talk about doing a bigger project."

I would have talked to mentors and friends about the challenges of two strangers starting a business together. The size and ambition of my dreams for the future would not have changed one iota, but the shape of my present would have. My start would have looked different.

Our contact at the church ended up being incredibly kind to me. She was as crushed as I was that the money was gone. She actually said that I didn't have to pay the remaining money back. But that didn't seem right, so my wife and I sent them a check for $2,310. I don't know if that's carrying-around cash for you—the kind of thing you use to buy cashmere socks when you want to treat yo'self—but at the Acuff house, that is some serious cake.

People always tell you that failure teaches you the best lessons, and that's true, but that doesn't mean I want to learn that way. Of the two options—lose $2,310 and learn a great lesson, or keep $2,310 and learn a great lesson—I know which one I'd pick. Don't be dumb like me. I implore you.

## DREAM HONESTLY

Be brutally realistic when you answer the question from the first chapter, "Where am I right now?" Answering that question honestly is critical to your career and maybe even your whole life.

In *Good to Great*, Jim Collins tells the story of Jim Stockdale, a US military officer who was held captive for eight years during the Vietnam War and tortured regularly. Collins asked Stockdale which soldiers didn't make it out. Stockdale answered,

> Oh, that's easy. The optimists. They were the ones who said, "We're going to be out by Christmas." And Christmas would come, and Christmas would go. They'd say, "We're going to be out by Easter." And Easter would come, and Easter would go. And then Thanksgiving, and then it would be Christmas again. And they died of a broken heart.
>
> This is a very important lesson. You must never confuse faith that you will prevail in the end—which you can never afford to lose—with the discipline to confront the most brutal facts of your current reality, whatever they might be.[3]

Avoid the temptation to believe that being honest about your current reality is somehow not the right way to dream big. Don't you dare be like my friends who say, "I've got $100,000 in student loans, but I'm going to pretend those don't exist and instead just dream about the future!" Honestly looking at where you currently are in life turns your present into a platform you can jump from instead of a prison that will hold you back. If you've got big bills, make big sacrifices at the start.

If you decided to have five kids in the first ten years of your marriage, don't then tell your family, "Daddy wants to dream. I'm going to quit my job, start an organic radish farm, and act like I'm a 19-year-old single guy with no responsibilities." Be honest about your present and turn it into a friend, like I should have with my approach to starting an ad agency.

This will not be easy because the world's definition of dreaming is just the opposite. People will say things like, "Step out in faith," or, "Follow your dreams and the universe will open doors for you where there were only walls." Those kinds of ideas make for amazing mugs but have a pretty horrible success rate. At best, those ideas are code for, "Don't make any plans," and at worst they are code for, "Abandon your current commitments."

You see the former in a million colorfully inspiring but ultimately empty sayings on Pinterest and Facebook. You see the latter exhibited in songs like John Mayer's "Walt Grace's Submarine Test, January 1967."

It's a beautiful song and such a great example of why John Mayer is a consummate storyteller (just not a good voicemail recording). In the lyrics, Mayer poetically describes the life of Walt Grace, a man who was "desperately hating this whole place." Walt decides to build a one-man submarine in his basement, "'cause when you're done with this world, you know the next is up to you." He succeeds against all odds and then rides the submarine all the way to Tokyo. It takes him weeks, but he does it! Hooray, dream fulfilled! Only there's a problem. Walt's a husband. Walt's a father of a few kids. In a song we may hail him as a dreamer, but in reality we'd call him an absentee father. When Mayer sings, "his wife told his kids he was crazy," it's nearly impossible to ignore the sadness of that picture—the picture of a man who was "done" with a world that included his wife and children, so he built a "home-made, fan-blade, one-man submarine ride."[4]

The world's definition of dreaming is often incredibly selfish. It involves ignoring everyone you know and love. Working on some private passion in the depths of your basement. Going off on an adventure without anyone else. And then weeks later letting people know you're not dead.

We tell that story in popular culture so often, we start to believe that dreaming or walking down the road to awesome is an inherently selfish idea. As if you only have two options: abandon every commitment you have and dream, or resign yourself to an average life in order to honor your commitments.

What if there was a third way? A way to honor all your commitments even while you completely change your life and the world in the process?

What if you don't have to be an absentee dad, a bad employee, or a failure of a spouse to chase a dream with more intensity than you can even imagine?

What if you could start today?

You can, regardless of your current circumstances. But first, you've got to deal with a very big wall.

(P.S. Starting with chapter 2, each chapter in this book will have a corresponding set of action steps in the back. You can find them on page 221. I thought about weaving them into the book but realized that would wreck the narrative flow. Like right now. Wasn't that last part all dramatic? "You've got to deal with a very big wall." It felt very "open the gates and seize the day," Newsies-style, to me. And then I had to ruin it with tactical, practical action steps. Okay, public service announcement over.)

# 3

# WHAT TO EXPECT WHEN YOU'RE STARTING

**THIS BOOK WOULD'VE BEEN A LOT EASIER TO WRITE** if I could just outline how I found my purpose. I'd use a bunch of words like *life force* and *destiny*. I'd pull out a few of those reverse sentences motivational speakers like me love: "Don't just dare to dream—dream to dare!" I'd get some sort of signature look, maybe a suit coat with a hood inexplicably sewn on the back and a watch you can only get in southern Norway. And then I'd go on some sort of "power up" tour around the country where I'd offer self-help advice like the back of a shampoo bottle.

> Find your true purpose.
> Be your true purpose.
> Live your purpose.
> Repeat as necessary.

And I'm not above that—let's be perfectly clear about that right now. I love books like that. They're not messy. And I tried to write that book telling you how to find your purpose, but I kept running into one big problem.

I didn't find my mine. I wish I had. As I mentioned, I went to Vietnam once, and that would have been pretty dramatic, especially because it's not one of the three big "find yourself in Europe countries" (Italy, England, France). But I didn't find it there.

My wife and I raised $60,000 to build two kindergartens there with help from the readers of my blog. When the schools were finished, we visited them. One hot afternoon in November, after the aforementioned run-in with the French motorcyclists, we stepped out of an old Land Cruiser into the front courtyard of a kindergarten.

There were hundreds of giggling children, dozens of parents, and a few chickens gathered for the opening ceremony. The local minister of education was there and promptly told me I looked like Prince William. He probably meant "skinny and pale," but my Vietnamese is no good so I'm going to assume he meant "tall and regal."

Before we went through the gates of the school, I stopped in the driveway and looked at the building. There were six class-rooms, a separate kitchen building, and a bathroom. I resisted the urge to immediately say, "In America, $30,000 wouldn't even buy you a nice Toyota Sequoia."

Instead I just stood there, in awe that a group of strangers on a blog had helped make this possible. I was content to leave it at that, to just cherish that moment like a Successories poster.

But out of nowhere, five words popped into my head. And they were the words that would forever ruin my ability to tell you how to find your perfect purpose in life:

*How did I get here?*

The truth is, I didn't know.

I could look back on the years leading up to the kindergartens and explain them in 20/20 hindsight, but the overwhelming reality was that I didn't know how I had come to be standing on a mountain in Vietnam.

I didn't know how blog readers had come together to change an entire village they'd never even heard of.

I didn't know how I'd landed halfway around the world to sit at a table while schoolchildren sang songs of celebration about finally having a school they could attend.

I didn't figure out my purpose and then execute it. I didn't write "Vietnam" on a whiteboard in Atlanta, scribble down "Nashville and Dave Ramsey," add "Write three books," then proceed to take deliberate steps to my very crystal clear finish line, finally crossing it exactly the way I planned all along.

It didn't happen that way. Not for me. And truly, not for most of us if we are honest. But when we talk about "finding our purpose," we think it will happen like clockwork, because most of us believe these lies about purpose:

## Everyone but you knows exactly what his is.

I don't know exactly what mine is. I have a rough sense of a handful of things I think are awesome, but I don't know my perfect purpose. There. Disproved that one. (I hope the rest are this easy.)

### You'll only have one.

I blame any romantic movie where someone is running in an airport for this belief. This is the "soulmate" concept of finding your purpose. You get one, and you'll just "know it when you know it." That and the amount of fireworks that will go off and the Natasha Bedingfield song you'll hear in the background will be your clue. Nonsense.

### You should have it figured out by the time you're 22 years old.

Sure you will. And your SAT score matters a lot too. I can't tell you how often my SAT score comes up as a 37-year-old. Seems like that's the first thing anyone wants to know. People are always saying to me, "Your job experience looks great, love your resume, good references, but when I say, 'Orange is to wrench as blue is to _____,' what does that mean to you?" Most people don't have their purpose figured out by 22.

### It changes everything instantly.

Your step will be lighter. Colors will seem brighter. Even food will taste different once you find your purpose. You know how you don't like the texture of strawberries? All those little bumpy things most people are able to ignore but you find disconcerting? Don't worry about them. As soon as you find your purpose, everything changes, including how strawberries feel in your mouth.

### You have to know the finish line before you cross the starting line.

In *The 7 Habits of Highly Effective People*, author Stephen Covey wrote that habit number two is "Begin with the end in mind."[1]

I completely agree. It's good to keep the end in mind. But since that book came out, we've mutated that thought into: "Begin with the end in stone." As if before you take a single step you have to know exactly what your final step will be. That's the biggest lie of all when it comes to finding your purpose.

The result of these lies is that most of us have forgotten something critical.

Purpose is not a final destination.

One of the worst things you can do is try to find your purpose in life. Nothing cripples you like trying to "find your purpose," or "figure out your dream," or "name your passion."

Regardless of the words you use, it's all nonsense and none of it ever works. Here's why:

## It puts tremendous pressure on you.

So all you need to do right now is sit down with a blank piece of paper or an empty journal and come up with the one idea that will guide the rest of your time on this planet? Awesome.

## It becomes an idol.

As soon as I find my purpose, the rest of my life will fall into place, my worries will vanish, and every morning I will bound out of bed with hope in my heart and jelly beans in my eyes.

## It stops you in your tracks.

Until you find your one true purpose, you can't get started on doing anything else. As soon as you get it, you'll start sprinting, but until then, stay right where you are.

For these reasons and more, I'm not a fan of "finding your purpose." I'm a fan of "living with purpose."

Living with purpose allows you to:

## Start today.

There's no waiting period. It's not a springboard. It's a filter for everything you encounter every day. Waiting to find your purpose tomorrow is a great way to ensure you don't live with purpose today.

## Start where you are.

You can live with purpose as a dad, as an employee, as a college student, as a friend, or as anything else.

## Start on what matters to you.

Why even pretend that you're going to find one thing and one thing only that you love doing for the rest of your life at the exclusion of all others? Don't get locked into a single purpose statement that suffocates you. Live with purpose and enjoy a thousand different passions as you continually walk the road to awesome.

The reality is that many scientists believe our brains aren't even done physically developing until we're in our mid-20s. Therefore, the idea that a 19-year-old is capable of choosing a perfect major and a perfect purpose that guides the next fifty years of their life is absurd.

And that's just your brain. What about your heart? What about your passions? What about your dreams? When do those stop developing? Your mid-30s? Your mid-50s? Hopefully never. So then why do we think we'll find a singular purpose that will guide us forever?

Forget finding a purpose. It's a never-ending story that will leave you empty. Live with purpose instead.

Get up and go to work with purpose. Handwrite three thank-you notes to employees today.

Play with your kids with purpose. Apply the same creativity and energy you use for projects at work to your playtime with your kids. Create "family goals" like "Walk my kids to school fifty times this year."

Love your spouse with purpose. Go on dates, don't wait for moments to reconnect to happen naturally, and encourage them with intentionality.

Vacation with purpose. Turn off your email for longer than twelve seconds and realize no one died during your absence.

Dream with purpose. Follow the action steps in the back of this book instead of just reading it and putting it right back on a shelf.

Whatever you're going to do, do it with purpose. Not as if purpose is a key you're going to find in the bottom of a trunk of old sweaters, but rather as if purpose is an approach to life that can shape everything you do.

## THE GREAT WALL

How will you know when you're living with purpose instead of trying to find purpose? When you stop worrying about the great wall of purpose. That may feel impossible at first because it's so massive. It stretches miles and miles in either direction. It's 1,000 feet tall and disappointingly close to the starting line.

It stands like a sentinel on the path to awesome. We can't dig under it. We can't scale it. We can't break through it. But there is a door right there in the middle of the wall. You can see the land of awesome through the keyhole. You can hear awesome if you put your ear against the door. You know awesome is just on the other side. But the great misconception is that you need a key to open the door. You don't.

The door is unlocked. You just need to turn the knob and walk through it.

That's the first secret about purpose. The door has been open the whole time. Push the door open and take the next step into awesome.

The second secret about purpose is that it usually finds you. Purpose is attracted to motion. Purpose is attracted to momentum. Purpose loves to surprise you mid-stride. Very rarely will it greet you on your front doorstep. More often than not, you'll encounter purpose in the middle of the road when you least expect it.

So start. The door has always been open.

But I must warn you. The moment you decide, "I'm going to live with purpose today instead of trying to find my purpose someday," you'll be tempted to look for shortcuts. Now that you are free to start down the path of Learning, you may want to turn that freedom into a license to jump ahead. Don't. It never works out.

## SHORTCUTS

I don't know about you, but I am exhausted. We escaped average. Took our first step toward awesome. Opened the door in the great wall of purpose. It's been an arduous few hours. And now we're on the edge of the land of Learning and the horizon looks massive.

Want to jump right over the first three destinations and land in Harvesting? Wouldn't you rather leap from the start straight into the land where it rains money? I would. And if you'd prefer that too, congratulations, you're human.

We all want a shortcut.

When confronted with work and a reward, we all would prefer the reward first or at least as soon as possible. But the path to awesome doesn't work that way. Ask any honest sage if they were an expert at something the first time they tried it, and they'll giggle and probably give you a caramel.

We all search for shortcuts. We all secretly hope there's a back door to our dreams. But there's not, even if you're Gwyneth Paltrow.

She is in the Mastering stage when it comes to acting. She's won an Oscar, been in more than twenty movies, and married somebody famous. I guess that last one doesn't make you a great actress, but it felt relevant somehow.

One day she decided she wanted to be a musician too. She signed a $900,000 recording deal with Atlantic, starred in a movie called *Country Strong*, played at the Country Music Awards, and planned her debut album.

Years later, the album is nowhere to be seen, *Country Strong* was a box-office failure, and Gwyneth isn't doing much singing. Why?

She's not yet a Master when it comes to music. Despite her money, despite her fame, despite her marriage to the front man of one of the most celebrated bands in the last twenty years, she didn't get to skip the lands of Learning and Editing. Whether your name is Gwyneth Paltrow or something that is considerably easier to spell, guess what? You've got to go through the Learning years of being a musician. You've got to go through the Editing years, too, if you really want to one day enter the lands of Mastering, Harvesting, and Guiding and be successful there.

Gwyneth Paltrow can't skip destinations on the map to awesome. You can't either. (And don't throw Bo Jackson at me. He played football and baseball his entire life. Those were parallel passions, not him deciding at 31 that he wanted to start a new one. And I will crush you with Bo in Tecmo Bowl.)

So if you've spent the last eight years being an accountant and having success at that and then you decide to be a writer, give yourself some grace. You may have been a great accountant, but if you want to be a writer, it's time to be 20 again.

The truth is, if you want to reach the land of Harvesting, if you want to be more awesome, more often, you have to go through the lands of Learning, Editing, and Mastering each time you pursue something new, whether it's a major pursuit or a minor one. You have to work hard and sacrifice and lean into your particular brand of awesome with energy and enthusiasm. Anytime you use the word *sacrifice* in a book, you should immediately offset it with something encouraging so people don't throw your book down and go play Wii Fit.

So here it is: You can't skip stages, but as I said earlier, you can accelerate them. There are four ways to shorten the amount of time you spend in each.

## 1. Start earlier.

In his best-selling book *Outliers,* Malcolm Gladwell references a study that Dr. K. Anders Ericsson conducted. Ericsson is a Swedish psychologist and Conradi Eminent Scholar and is recognized as one of the world's leading researchers on the science of expertise. Gladwell wrote about the "10,000-hour rule," an idea that Ericsson put forth that states that expertise takes 10,000 hours of practice to achieve (roughly twenty hours a week for ten years).[2] So then why, as Gladwell profiled, did Bill Gates become Bill Gates or Tiger Woods become Tiger Woods? In part because they started earlier than other people. Tiger had a golf club in his hand when he was a toddler. Gates started programming computers at the age of 13. By the time he was 6, Mozart had practiced an estimated 3,500 hours.[3] Turns out the shortcut to greatness isn't a shortcut at all. You just start earlier than everybody else. As a result, you are able to reach Editing, Mastering, and Harvesting much sooner in life. It was no fluke that Woods won The Masters by a preposterous twelve strokes when he was only 21 years old. He'd been Learning, Editing, and Mastering golf for eighteen years by then.

## 2. Stand on the shoulders of giants.

I'm more comfortable onstage as a public speaker than I should be based on the limited amount of experience I've had, and that's because of my dad. He's a pastor, and I spent eighteen years watching him preach. For almost two decades, he showed me how fun and normal it was to stand up in front of hundreds of people and share ideas with them. I didn't teach myself how to be calm onstage—my dad taught me that, and I'm standing on his shoulders.

If your dad was a professional baseball player and raised you in the locker room, you'll have a head start on a baseball career if that's the path you want to take. You'll grow up understanding the game in a way most people won't. If you build on his foundation, you may get to the land of Harvesting a lot faster than other people.

If you've got a parent, mentor, boss, or friend who cleared the way for you, you may be able to stand on the shoulders of a giant. And as Andy Stanley says, you'll go "further, faster" than you would have on your own.

## 3. Work harder and smarter.

I've never met a farmer who was surprised by his crops. Who stood on a front porch, in overalls I'm assuming, and stared out at a crop of blood oranges when he clearly remembered planting soybeans. If you work hard, you tend to expect results. If you decide that you'll spend ten hours a week on your path to expertise instead of twenty, you'll get there slower than someone who owns the twenty and gets down to business. If you now want to tweet out, "Hard work pays off, new thought by @jonacuff," feel free.

## 4. Harvest someone else's fields.

Gladwell didn't throw out the 10,000-hour rule as the definitive reason that Bill Gates became Bill Gates. In fact, he argued that "the biggest misconception about success is that we do it solely on our smarts, ambition, hustle, and hard work."[4] If Gates hadn't had access to a computer when he was 13, it may have been difficult for him to accumulate 10,000 hours so quickly. He had opportunities other people didn't necessarily have. Or in other words, he harvested fields he did not plant.

That happens sometimes in life. You get an opportunity that is beyond what your experience years would dictate. Someone takes a shot on you. Against all logic, a boss believes in you and risks a project under your young lead. A friend has a connection at a record label, and in one relational leap you clear the dozens of hurdles it usually takes for someone to hear your demo.

There will be moments when you get to harvest someone else's field and shorten a stage or two. We often call this someone's "big break." That's happening to me right now. When he hired me, Dave Ramsey took me from speaking to crowds of 100 to crowds of 10,000 almost overnight. I didn't earn my way to that opportunity. Dave spent twenty years building his stage and then graciously invited me to join him on it. When I speak at a Dave Ramsey live event, that's his harvest that he's generously decided to share with me.

Did I plant the fields Dave is letting me harvest right now? Nope. That was a finish line I couldn't have possibly predicted. Did I come up with the vision to have new brands like me at his company? Nope. Did I, through my hard work, make Dave a generous leader who is humble enough to share the stage with someone who technically hasn't earned it? Nope.

But guess where I was when Dave invited me to think about joining his team? At his office. I'd driven up for the third time in two years to speak there. For free. I'd spent years building a brand. I'd spent years writing a blog and a book. I'd spent years hustling and working as hard as I possibly could in the lands of Learning and Editing. Dave didn't knock on my front door and say, "I've never heard of you, but I'm here to change your life with an incredible opportunity." I'd already kicked down the door of purpose and started traveling the road of awesome when I met Dave. He met me when I was already in motion. My relationship with Dave wasn't a by-product of luck. *Luck* is a word people who are lazy use to describe people who are hustling. If you ever taste it in your mouth, spit it out as fast as you can.

At first glance, two of those ways to accelerate awesome should make you hate me at least a little. "Great! All I have to do to be awesome is start my dream when I was a toddler! Fantastic. I'll get a time machine. And I need my dad to have been a successful member of the same exact industry I'm curious about. Thanks for the help, Jon!"

That's not what I'm saying at all. You don't need to go back in time to be awesome; you just have to start right now. Regretting that you didn't start earlier is a great distraction from moving on your dream today, and the reality is that today is earlier than tomorrow. As far as having a mom or dad who showed you the ropes, or a giant in your life, that's fixable too. You'd be surprised how easy it is to find a giant, someone who is farther down the path than you. People who are awesome are usually surprisingly willing to share their wisdom if you ask humbly.

You may not be able to skip stages, but you'd be amazed what a difference hustle, hard work, and the steps we'll discuss in this book can make in your ability to shorten them.

Just make sure that while you're hustling you don't start thinking you deserve more than you really do.

## THE ENTITLEMENT TRAP

When it comes to conference speakers, there are two kinds:

1. Important people
2. People who get interviewed onstage

Important people are generally great speakers who have done great things. Malcolm Gladwell, for instance, is an important person. You may know him. I've already quoted him twice in this book and will probably proceed to do so forty-seven more times. He's great at the craft of speaking and has written some of the best business books of the last fifteen years.

The second category of conference speaker is someone who has done something amazing but may not be a great public speaker. Josh Hamilton, for instance, falls into this category. When he was on the main stage at the Catalyst Conference, a 13,000-person leadership conference in Atlanta, he was interviewed. He's done something great—he came back from drug addiction to become a Major League All-Star—but he's not a professional public speaker. That's not his gift.

I like to think I'm in the first category—that I am an important person—but occasionally conference organizers remind me that I am not. Via email mostly.

While I was writing this book, I found out that a conference I was going to keynote at downgraded me to interview level. Now, clearly that's okay because I have some wicked awesome stories to talk about from the time I hit a walk-off grand slam to beat the Yankees—I love talking about hitting some dingers!—but it's disappointing nonetheless.

Upon receiving this news, that I am interview level and not important-people level, I wanted to respond to the email with: "Are you kidding me? Interviews are for celebrities who hate public speaking but have a compelling story that the world is dying to know. Interviews are for people who are unproven on the mic and can't be trusted with the stage. Interviews are the training wheels of public speaking. I'm doing wheelies, son. Front and back! I'm ready!"

Except, I'm not. I spoke professionally for the first time in 2008. Since then, I've done it approximately 100 times. Sure, I've had a few big moments, like speaking to 10,000 people at a college, but is anyone who has only done something 100 times really a master?

If I'm being honest, I'm still in the land of Learning when it comes to public speaking. (If you're booking me to speak, please don't let this honesty confuse you into paying me a smaller fee.) I'm only in my 20s when it comes to rocking the mic. And therein lies the greatest temptation most of us will face as we reside in the land of Learning.

We want to enter Harvesting without traveling through Learning, Editing, or Mastering.

It only takes a few steps into the land of Learning for you to spot your first entitlement ladder. It's leaning there with your name on it. "Come on over," it whispers. "You've worked hard enough; here's a ladder to climb to the top immediately. This is your time!"

I get that—I do. I don't really want to learn how to be a great public speaker. I don't really want to spend hours editing that skill. I don't want to spend time mastering it. I just want to do it a few times, have everyone recognize me as a master, and then enjoy the rewards.

Why do we think we can skip thirty years of life experience? I think there are a lot of reasons, but here are three really obvious ones:

## 1. The Internet has changed our definition of *expert.*

In 2012, a group called Invisible Children came out with a viral video about Ugandan warlord Joseph Kony. There was a lot of opposition to their social justice mission, and one of the sources quoted often was a blog called *Visible Children*. Was the author of this blog—whom media sources linked to as an expert—a grizzled professor of Ugandan studies? A man in his 60s who had lived in Uganda before returning to the United States to write books about the unique challenges and opportunities the country faced? No, the author of the blog was a college sophomore from Canada. Beseeched by media inquiries, he had to write posts on his blog that said, "I'm a second-year political science student, not an expert, and the audience for this post was a group of approximately thirty friends to whom it was emailed originally."[5] And, "Today I've turned down media requests from Al Jazeera English, FOX, NBC's *Today* show, and BBC World Service. Why? Because *my opinion* isn't what's relevant."[6]

What an honest response, but it does reveal a shift in our culture. Twenty years ago, do you know whom the BBC didn't contact for expert opinions on geopolitical issues in war-torn African countries? Sophomores at Acadia University in Nova Scotia.

## 2. We celebrate accomplishment-free celebrities.

It's impossible to go to the grocery store and not be confronted with magazines promoting people who are famous for being famous. The message is simple: you don't have to do anything to be considered important. Sure, we've had gossip magazines and starlets like Marilyn Monroe for decades, but Marilyn Monroe was also in twenty-nine movies. She was famous because she made movies.

## 3. Everything else in life is instant.

If you ever played Little League sports, then at least fourteen times your coach asserted, "You play like you practice." If you spend eighteen hours goofing off and halfheartedly exercising during practice, you can't suddenly flip a switch and be amazing during the game that week. Your practice determines how you play. This is true of almost every facet of life. So what are we practicing right now as a culture? Everything should be instant. That's the rallying cry of smartphone manufacturers. "It's the fastest 4G! Your brand-new phone is already so ten seconds ago!" And as soon as you reach fast, you want faster right away, because your definition never stops changing.

When I was in college, I actually said this sentence fairly regularly: "I wasn't able to get on the Internet today." I said that sentence because it was true. Connecting to the Internet was this difficult, crazy, chirp-filled experience. And if you were fortunate enough to get on, you were constantly afraid that you were about to get kicked off. That AOL would unexpectedly tell you "Goodbye!" before you were ready, forcing you to start the whole process again. It was the technology version of cranking a Ford Model-T. Now? If my smartphone doesn't pick up four bars of service in the jungles of Brazil, I am enraged. Comedian Louis C.K. summarizes this expectation with the retort he uses when people are mad that their smartphone isn't operating quickly. He says, "Give it a second! It's going to space! Can you give it a second to get back from space?"[7]

Every day we have the belief that good things should be delivered quickly. Of course our careers and lives and purposes should happen at the same rate. It'd be ridiculous to think they'd take time!

If you live with those three beliefs long enough, you start to feel you're entitled to being an expert immediately. You start to believe that you deserve to enter the land of Harvesting just after college—even during college, if you play your cards right. That you have the right to skip the lands of Learning, Editing, and Mastering. That you're ready for a main-stage speaking spot, not just an interview.

You're not. I'm not either. And that's okay, because I've climbed the entitlement ladder a dozen times, and let me tell you where it leads . . . nowhere.

You just climb and climb and climb, each rung taking you farther away from reality and what it really takes to reach awesome. Your whole perception of the world changes from up there. Other people look really tiny and insignificant. Like pesky ants who are just in the way. They don't understand you. They're unable to grasp the full scope of your greatness, but from high on the ladder it all makes sense.

The great peril of the entitlement ladder is that it never ends. It doesn't stop. You just keep climbing and climbing until the air gets so thin and your judgment so skewed that you eventually yell the sentence you used to make fun of people for saying: "Do you know who I am?" And when someone says, "Do you know who I am?" what they're really saying is, "Do you know who I am? Because I don't. I lost sight of that person a long time ago."

Don't climb a single rung up the entitlement ladder. Demanding something you haven't truly earned is a great way to get stuck in the land of Learning for decades, even an entire lifetime. Kick those ladders over and keep walking.

You can shorten your journey with hard work, but the entitlement ladder will lead you nowhere.

## IGNORE THE VOICES

Stories without dragons are boring.

You don't get "happily ever after" unless at some point it was in doubt, unless the whole adventure was in question. Success was anyone's guess. Survival was up for grabs.

A hero without a villain isn't really a hero. Superman without Lex Luthor would have just been "Man," and that would have made for a really dull movie.

But rest assured, this story has a villain too. This story has a dragon.

You knew it had to. As we discussed in the first section of this book, awesome is simple. The path is not complicated. The plan is not complex. So then why haven't you and I spent more time being awesome thus far in life?

We probably got stuck in the forest of voices.

One day, in a 1920s cabin next to a train track and Norman Rockwell houses, my friend Al Andrews asked me a question.

Al runs a nonprofit called Porter's Call in Franklin, Tennessee. About ten years ago, he recognized that a lot of the clients who came to his counseling practice were musicians. Some of them were in desperate need of a safe place to restore their stories but couldn't afford traditional counseling. Others were selling tens of millions of records and needed a place where they could be themselves, not the idea or image of themselves that everyone sees on the Grammys.

So Al met with the record labels in Nashville and told them, "Look: you're spending millions of dollars creating these superstar musicians. You're surrounding them with musical talent, stylists, designers, and support staff. But then their lives fall apart in the process. What if you sponsored Porter's Call and it became a place where musicians and their families could receive free counseling?"

The labels loved the idea, and so for the last decade, Al has been creating a safe haven for artists. It's an amazing bit of geography in a city that otherwise tends to grind musicians up.

My dad went to college with Al, so he lets me slide around the "Must be a musician on a record label to go to Porter's Call" rule. One afternoon, Al asked me, "What do your voices tell you?"

I thought that was kind of a crazy question and considered answering it with counseling jargon I've learned in the last few years:

"My parents didn't hug me enough."

"I'd like to learn how to do some reflective listening."

"Can we spend this session unpacking some of my father wounds?"

I decided instead to answer his question with a question of my own, so I asked Al what he meant.

He got quiet for a few seconds and probably scratched his beard thoughtfully, because that's what therapists in movies are always doing. Then he said, "Well, I've asked thousands of people that question over the years, and I've learned something: no one has a positive internal voice. No one's internal voice tells them, 'You're skinny enough. You sure are pretty. People are going to love that new project you're working on. It's going to be a huge success.' Which makes me curious about what your voices are telling you.

"Most of us tend to think they're telling us the truth. We've heard them for so long that we trust them. We think they're looking out for us, that they've got our best in mind. That they're trying to protect us or help us. We think our voices are friends, but they're not. They're foes."

I walked out that afternoon without an answer. I drove home thinking about that question, "What do my voices tell me?"

For weeks, the question haunted me. I didn't write any emo poetry about it or tattoo it in tribal font on my wrist, but it stayed with me.

In order to shake it, I decided to do something really simple. I decided to write down the messages of my voices. I wasn't going to go on a vision quest or fight a she-bear, but I could at least listen for the voices and write them down if I had any.

The first one I heard was pretty obvious.

For years and years, every morning I've heard the same question in my head and my heart. One of my voices always asks,

"Are you happy enough?" It's a small question, but the conversation it causes is anything but small.

VOICE: Are you happy enough?

ME: I'm pretty happy. I'm not happy all the time. I mean, sometimes I'm sad.

VOICE: Whoa! You're not happy all the time? You're working your dream job right now. You write and speak for a living. You work for Dave Ramsey! If you're not happy all the time right now, I don't know if you'll ever be happy.

ME: Yikes! That kind of makes me unhappy just thinking about it. What should I do to fix that?

VOICE: Maybe there's something you can do perfectly today that will make you perfectly happy.

ME: Good idea. Which thing?

VOICE: Hard to say. Better play it safe and just do everything perfectly today.

ME: I have to be perfect all day? That's a lot of pressure. That kind of makes me unhappy.

*Spin, spin, spin.*

Before I know it, my best creativity, best time, and best energy have been commandeered by this voice. And it's not the only voice. There are many I hear throughout the days and weeks of my journey.

They are the voices of fear and doubt, and they are governed by a simple truth: they only get loud when you do work that matters. Want to stay on the road to average? Want to rock vanilla right to the grave? Okay, fear and doubt will leave you alone.

However, with the very first step you take on the road of awesome, fear and doubt stir from their slumber. The minute the purpose door creaks on its hinges and you push it open, the pointy ears of fear and doubt perk up. Continue on the road to awesome, and fear and doubt begin whispering lies and confusing statements meant to get you back on the average, safe path. But you should know that these voices are not unique. In fact, they convey pretty much the same three messages to every person who dares start down the road to awesome.

## 1. Who are you to do that?

The second you choose to be more awesome, fear will ask you a question: "Who are you to do that?"

Fear doesn't care what your particular "that" is. You could be starting a business or quitting a job. You could be writing a book or becoming a nanny. Doesn't matter to fear. The specifics never do. Regardless of what you want to do or who you are, fear will always see you as wholly unqualified for anything you ever dream or attempt.

Even the slightest step toward awesome will cause fear to fire into your heart like a warning flare.

"Who are you to do that?"

"What makes you think you can be that?"

"You don't have the right education, background, or experience to do that."

"You're just a mom or a customer call center representative."

"None of your previous life experiences apply in any manner to this new dream."

The first argument from fear is that you're not qualified, and it's the one I experienced when I wrote my third book, *Quitter*. My first book was a Christian satire, and *Quitter* was going to be a business book. Fear was quick to point that out. Here's what one of my voices said:

"You can't write a book like *Quitter*! Your first book doesn't even count. You've never even written a 'real book.' That was just some dumb blog that got turned into a book. It's a collection of loosely tied-together essays, and it's illustrated! There's a unicorn prancing through a field of flowers. You didn't write a book; you published a coloring book. Who do you think you are to write a business book? What makes you think you can jump shelves? You can't go from the Christian Inspiration section to the Business section. You're the funny Christian guy. That's who you are, and no one will ever believe differently. How dare you dream that you could write a business book. No one is going to believe this."

And I believed the voice. The writing process was torturous, and even after it came out I struggled with that voice.

One day my team leader called me into his office and asked me why I was apologizing for *Quitter*. I didn't know what he meant, so he explained further.

"Do you believe in *Quitter*? Do you believe it's a good book that people need to read? Do you believe it can help someone change their life?"

I responded slowly, but my answer was yes.

"Then you've got to start talking about it. You've practically been apologizing for it, sheepishly sharing about it online and ignoring it. Be brave enough to admit you wrote a good book. Believe in it. Quit apologizing."

He was right. The voice I'd listened to wasn't a friend. It was a foe. And in trying to knock me off course, it showed its colors.

If you manage to wrestle through feeling wildly unqualified to do something awesome, fear will change tactics and hand you a calendar.

## 2. You're too late.

It was 7:27 a.m. on a Monday. I was sitting in my office at home, in front of the bookshelves my wife reorganized by color. I was trying to write a little, but a chorus of voices filled my head. This is what they were saying:

*You're behind.*

*You'll never get ahead.*

*If you could just get ahead, then you could rest.*

*It's too late.*

*If you had more time, you could get it all done.*

Like most of the other voices I struggle with, this was not a new one. But on that morning, for the first time, I decided it might be a lie.

So instead of spinning out, I started to write out what each thought really meant:

"You're behind."

Behind what? According to what schedule? Against what measurement? What does that even mean? There is no clock I am on right now. Work hasn't even started yet. I am not in a race. There is no competitor I am fighting against. What am I behind?

"You'll never get ahead."

Ahead of what? What does *ahead* mean? Who is defining *ahead*? I have a sneaking suspicion that *ahead* doesn't exist.

"If you could just get ahead, then you could rest."

Rest is a gift, not a reward. It's not a hobby that lazy people take advantage of; it's woven into the fabric of our very biology. The body is designed to rest. I don't have to earn that with my performance. Rest is not a by-product of my success; it's a by-product of my humanity. I don't have to get ahead to enjoy it or need it.

"It's too late."

Ridiculous. It's Monday morning at 7:27. How is it already too late this week? I couldn't have more week ahead of me if I tried. I refuse to accept that the minute I wake up on Monday morning it's already "too late."

"If you had more time, you could get it all done."

Nonsense. My definition of *all* would just grow. And why is "done" a goal? If you discover something you love doing, you don't want to be done. You want to do it every day. Done is dead.

After a few minutes of writing, the absurdity of fear's view of time started to come to light. And it is absurd, because fear tries to tell you two things about time: "Do it later" or "It's too late."

The first delays you with laziness. The second destroys you with regret.

And neither is true.

Unless you're dead right now, it's not too late. Don't give credence to the calendar fear and doubt want to show you. It's incredibly heavy and never includes a page for "today." Fear and doubt's calendar always starts with yesterday or tomorrow.

You've got today, and today is all you need to start. The rest will come into view as you go.

## 3. It has to be perfect.

As I mentioned earlier, fear and doubt are schizophrenic. Their favorite thing to do is argue both sides of the coin so that you don't have a side to stand on. They love to tell you, "It will never work," and, "It has to be perfect."

The first thought tells you that no part of your dream will succeed. The second thought tells you that every part of it *must* succeed. That doesn't make even a little bit of sense, but you will hear both voices.

This one is pretty easy to defeat. The reality is that since the dawn of time there hasn't been a single situation fear thought would work. If you ask fear if something is going to work, the answer will always be no.

Fear would have told the Wright Brothers not to fly. Fear would have told Rosa Parks to change seats. Fear would have told Steve Jobs that people hate touchscreens.

Don't even ask it for advice. You know its answer. Just move on.

Those are the three most common messages, but you will hear others. I've asked thousands of people what their voices tell them, and they've had thousands of different answers.

I once asked a group of youth ministers what their voices told them. They told me things like:

"You work with kids; you'll always be a kid; you'll never be a real man."

"You never went to seminary—who are you to teach kids?"

I asked a group of men what their voices told them, and a guy in the front row shouted out, "Wait until your father gets home."

He was in his mid-50s. He hadn't lived at home for thirty years, and yet that fear still rang loudly in his head.

If you don't deal with your voices, they don't go away. They don't naturally get smaller.

Doubt and fear are like muscles. Every time you believe a lie about yourself, it gets easier to believe it the next time. If you listen to your voices for the next ten years, they'll only be stronger in ten years. They'll get louder and closer to the surface. They'll need less proof to pop up and get all mouthy.

Simply put, if you don't kill your voices, they will kill you.

But we're not going to let that happen. We're not going to become emotional hoarders, storing up anger and bitterness before eventually moving to Florida and assuming that everyone is out to get us and our little dog.

We're going to beat our voices by doing two things:

## 1. Documenting them.

Voices are invisible bullies, and they hate when you make them visible. The best way to do that is to dress them up with words. To write them down in a simple notebook. They can't stand to be documented, because the minute they are, you can see how stupid they are. Lies hate the light of day.

Every time you take a step toward being awesome and a voice gets loud, write it down. Don't ask, "Is this a voice?" before you do. Just write. Fast and furious and imperfectly. Scribble as many as you can down, and then refute them with truth, like I did with the ones that told me I was too late and already behind. That's step one.

## 2. Sharing our voices.

Do you know what fear and doubt fear? Community. One of fear and doubt's chief aims is to make you feel alone. Like you're the only one who feels a certain way. Fear wants to isolate you and put you on an island. As long as you keep your fear to yourself, no one can tell you the truth about it.

No one can reflect back to you that you are lying to you. No one can admit they feel the same way too. No one can help you see what is really going on. No one can encourage you.

So if you're going to tell your voices, "Kick rocks, punk," you've got to share them with other people.

Now, this is clearly a pretty easy thing to do. You're going to want to roll up to Starbucks, order a skinny extra hot Venti Vanilla Latte, and when the barista asks, "Do you want your receipt?" say, "No, I don't need my receipt. What I need is to stop listening to these voices in my head that tell me there are already too many professional photographers in the world. Am I right? Do you hear voices too? No? Okay, I'll just pay for my coffee and this Jason Mraz World Music CD bundle then. Thanks."

It's not easy to find folks to share your voices with. At the conferences I throw, we do that as an exercise. We do a whole session on it, and the tenor of the room changes as people start to realize they're not alone and that everyone has the same doubts and fear.

You've got to tell your close friends or family or a counselor about your voices. The exact person will be different for everyone who reads this book, but never waste time trying to battle a voice alone. In some cases that voice of fear and doubt will have had a ten-year head start on you. Don't go it alone.

## FINAL THOUGHTS ON FEAR

At its worst, the forest of voices is an insatiable black hole, gobbling up our time, our energy, and our hope.

At its best, it is a compass. As Steven Pressfield says, it can "point to true North . . . that calling or action it most wants to stop us from doing."[8]

Start. And as you pass through the wall of purpose, kick over the ladder of entitlement, and fight back against the voices of fear and doubt, the map to awesome will become a little clearer. The next steps will not be easy, but they will become increasingly rewarding as you stay the course.

# 4

# LEARNING

**SAVE FOR THE COST OF THIS BOOK** (which I hope was paid for in full and then promptly reviewed on Amazon), the road to awesome will not cost you any money. Whether you have a nickel to your name or a billion-dollar empire, you can walk this road.

But the road is not free. It actually costs you a different currency—in fact, the most expensive currency there is: time.

Every land you walk through, from Learning to Guiding, will require deposits of your time. But instead of waiting for more time to magically appear in your day, you're going to launch a rescue mission of your current days. That starts right now.

## ALL WE NEED IS THIRTY

Recognizing that time was a fuel that moved me down the road, I immediately tried to go from zero to 1,000 mph overnight. That's not really surprising. Remember the all-or-nothing voice? The one that tells you "Don't do it" or "Do it all perfectly"? That one gets loud again when you start to be deliberate about how you spend your time.

The second you think seriously about finding more time in your day or week to work on being more awesome more often, fear will tell you to make sure every second of your day is perfectly mapped out. It will try to get you to pick up a complicated time-management system or, in my case, a sword.

SWORD stood for:

**Serve**
**Worship**
**Order**
**Rest**
**Dance**

I decided that every day, all day, I would be making sure my activities fell into one of those five categories. If I was at work, that counted as serving time. Write it down. If I was sleeping, look at all the rest minutes I was racking up! Write it down. If I was exercising, that was dance time. (That's what happens when you try to come up with an acronym. At least one of the letters in every acronym is going to be hit with the ugly stick. I promise I auditioned fifty other D-words until I was forced to go with *dance*.)

I carried a little notebook around with me, constantly checking off my minutes to make sure I was using the SWORD that would blaze my path to more awesome more often. I wrote multiple, fairly pretentious blog posts about it to tell everyone this amazing plan I had discovered. I was a laser of ridiculousness, regularly asking my wife things like, "Well, I played with the kids outside, which was kind of exercise, so that's Dance; but I was serving them as well, as their dad. Do you think those six minutes count as Dance or Serve? Should I create a category called SANCE that marries the two?" At which point my wife would slam her head in a drawer a few times.

I gave up on the whole SWORD system after a month and promptly got right back to wasting all my time. I only had two speeds: waste all my time or try to be impossibly perfect with my time.

What I learned in that season was that when it comes to time management, or most other ways to accelerate awesome, change has to be simple. Especially new change. It has to be easily manageable, or we'll fail at it before we even start. We can add on other changes down the road, but when we're beginning our journey, we just need to get one thing right. One tiny taste of progress. The mountain can wait. It's been there for years and will still be there tomorrow. We don't have to scale it all at once. We don't have to rescue our entire year at the onset of the journey.

In fact, all we have to do is find thirty minutes in our week. One half hour is all I'm asking you to give at the start. This simple sacrifice was the biggest, most important thing I did to change my career. I can say without a shadow of a doubt if I hadn't found those thirty minutes, I never would have written four books. I wouldn't have moved to Nashville for my dream job with Dave Ramsey. And I wouldn't have made it through the land of Learning. Thirty minutes. That's all you're going to rescue, and fortunately, I know where to find yours.

## BE SELFISH AT 5:00 A.M.

You're too busy to be awesome right now. Whether it's a book or a blog or a project at work or a new job, life is probably too full to really work tirelessly on your "thing."

You've got a lot going on. I do too. And sometimes, when we focus on our dreams and try to take steps down the path of awesome, our wives cry in the kitchen. That's been my experience, anyway.

One Tuesday during a holiday break, I spent four hours writing a book idea. My kids were occupied with new Christmas presents and my wife was straightening up the house. At about three in the afternoon, I resurfaced from our home office and talked to my wife in the kitchen.

Her words were short and quick. I asked her what was wrong and she immediately replied, "I thought we were going to spend the day together." Then she started crying.

In that moment and many others, I failed to follow a simple rule of awesomeness. I was selfish at the wrong time of the day. Those hours—in the middle of the day during Christmas vacation—weren't really mine. When you're a spouse, parent, or caregiver, your time doesn't just belong to you. It's in large part communal property, shared by the entire house.

But that doesn't mean you can't be selfish with some of that time. You just have to know when you can be, which is why I mention 5:00 a.m.

The mornings I get up and write from 5:00 to 5:30, you'd be surprised at how infrequently my wife tells me I've been ignoring her. You'd be shocked at how rarely my oldest daughter wants me to watch her jump rope before the sun breaks the horizon.

You may even be mystified at how seldom my youngest daughter asks to go bike riding at 5:15 a.m.

You can be selfish at 5:00 a.m. Or 11:00 p.m. if your spouse goes to bed early and staying up an extra thirty minutes doesn't wreck your next day. You can also rescue thirty minutes during lunch. Last I checked, you don't need a full hour to eat a turkey sandwich, even if the cheese is organic, gluten-free, udder-to-table cheese. The point is that you can carve out time in your day and claim it, if you're willing to hustle.

If you're not married or don't have kids, this idea still applies. Your time is still shared, especially if you have a full-time job. Your boss may never cry in your arms in the kitchen on the day after Christmas. That would be weird. But if you're selfish with the wrong hours, your boss may indeed say to you, "Hey, last I checked, we were paying you to do work for us. Am I off base here?"

We all have commitments we have to keep. In one form or another, we all have spouses with expectations that should be met. We also have dreams that need attention.

To start, just be selfish at 5:00 a.m.

And if you don't like the word *selfish*, then rewrite that idea. I won't be offended. Call it your "get furious at five" mandate.

Whatever words you want to use, rescue thirty minutes to walk down your path to awesome. If you can't—if the idea of setting your alarm thirty minutes earlier sounds horrible to you—then you may not be ready for awesome.

If your dream isn't worth thirty minutes, you've either got the wrong dream or you're just pretending you have one. If the minimum you're willing to pay in order to be awesome is less than thirty minutes, you'd better go back to average. Nobody gets up early on the road to average. Nobody stays up late on the road to average. You can sleep in to your heart's content or watch late-night TV until the infomercials begin to make perfect sense. Either way, you're safe on the average road.

## ONE REASON 5:00 A.M. TENDS TO DOMINATE 11:00 P.M.

"I'm a night owl!" is often the excuse people give me when I encourage them to get up early and work on their dream.

I think that's a fair push back. I think there are probably some people who may be predisposed to going to bed later than others. But after hearing that response from so many of my friends over the years, I decided to see if my belief about the importance of mornings could be backed up by research. Maybe even with science. Here's what I found:

Willpower tends to favor the morning.

In a well-known 1996 research project led by Roy Baumeister at Case Western Reserve University, scientists had two groups of people sit down in a room. One group was told that they could eat the warm chocolate-chip cookies in the bowl in front of them. They just had to ignore the other bowl, which was full of radishes. The next group was told just the opposite. Eat the radishes; resist the cookies. After the experiment, researchers came back in the room and told the participants they needed to tabulate the results. Would they mind waiting around? While they were waiting, they could try to solve this simple puzzle. Only the puzzle wasn't all that simple. It actually had no solution— the scientists just wanted to see how long each person would attempt to solve it.

Can you guess what happened? The people who had to eat the radishes and resist the cookies tried an average of about eight minutes before they gave up and quit. The people who ate the cookies tried an average of about nineteen minutes. Why? It appears that willpower is finite. We have a limited supply of it. The people who ate the radishes and fought back the desire to eat the warm cookies were out of willpower. Their supply was depleted. They didn't want to do the puzzle. The people who ate the cookies? They had a full supply. They were willing to try more than twice as long. In his book *The Power of Habit*, Charles Duhigg describes how this study helps shed light on things like executives having affairs at night. After a stressful day of being on, making difficult decisions, fighting, and leading, executives have very little left in the tank.[1] This suggestion by researchers is by no means a justification for bad behavior, but it does give us a better understanding of how we are wired.

Have you ever had a task or activity that if you didn't do it in the morning it didn't happen when you got home from work? If you missed your jog at 6:00 a.m., after a day at the office and a long commute home, there was very little chance it would happen at 6:00 p.m.—even if you were single and lived alone. You may have thought you were being lazy, but what if you'd simply spent your willpower for that day?

In the book *The Way We're Working Isn't Working*, Tony Schwartz further explains Roy Baumeister's analysis of the cookie-versus-radish test:

In short, we each have one reservoir of will and discipline, and it is depleted by *any* act of conscious self-regulation—whether that's resisting a cookie, solving a puzzle, or doing anything else that requires effort. "The implication," Baumeister writes, "is that many widely different forms of self-control draw on a common resource, or self-control strength, which is quite limited and hence can be depleted readily."[2]

Don't start getting up earlier on your road to awesome just because it worked in my life.

Get up earlier because you want the best shot at success.

Get up earlier because you want access to your best willpower.

Get up earlier because you want the way your brain works and the way your physiology reacts to be your friend, not your foe.

## THE FIVE-STEP SECRET TO GETTING IT ALL DONE

You rescued thirty minutes. You put your television and video watching on a diet. You are starting to hustle. You're making time for all the different things you want to learn about right now. And the truth is, you're going to be really busy.

We all are.

There are hundreds of things I need to cross off my to-do list each day. Respond to emails. Attend meetings. Return phone calls. Answer text messages. Pick up the kids from gymnastics and art. Finish work projects. Start home projects.

I realized one day that my list was getting longer and my days felt like they were getting shorter. I was having trouble getting it all done.

In order to survive, I came up with a five-step secret to getting it all done. If you're busy too, feel free to use it:

1. Admit that you can't possibly get it all done.

2. Give yourself the grace to accept that as reality, not failure.

3. Do the things you can do with your full attention.

4. Celebrate what happens during Step 3 instead of obsessing over the things you didn't get to.

5. Repeat as necessary.

That's it. I was thinking about turning that list into an app, but checking it off would just be one more thing you'd have to do each day. Instead, just tear out these pages. Put the list on your fridge or whatever the more relevant appliance is, and start on step 1. If you can get that one done, you're 99 percent of the way there and will have a much better grasp on being more awesome more often.

## THE PLANE CRASH

Just beyond the forest of voices, where fear first got loud on the road to awesome, you'll stumble upon a plane crash. And while most of us would walk by with only that shameful curiosity we feel when we pass a car accident on the highway, if we're going to be awesome we may need to stop and take a closer look. Since we've just rescued thirty minutes, we've got the time.

I took a closer look a few years ago and, to tell you the truth, I always wanted to be in a plane crash. Not one of those jarring ones in the mountains where you have to eat the people who didn't survive. That's gross. I just wanted a section of the roof to come off, have some carry-on bags that were too big in the first place fly out the gaping hole, and then land safely and take a quick ride on the most exclusive slide in the world.

I'd save a few people from a fireball of some sort, jump down that big yellow inflatable wonder, and then wander in a cornfield or float in a shark-free portion of the balmy Caribbean Sea for a few hours. Then I'd do a couple of interviews, maybe go on *Letterman* in a smart-looking sweater, and write a book.

Best of all, I'd have something that near-death experiences always seem to deliver—a reason to live.

No one ever survives a plane crash and then says, "Really made me want to watch more television. When your life flashes before your eyes, you start to realize how you've been taking shows about cake for granted."

Nope, they say things like: "My life will never be the same again. I hug longer, smell more flowers, and can taste capers in a way that you non-near-death-experience people will never understand."

And so in my quest to find meaning, I thought that might be a great shortcut.

The trouble is, it's not easy to get in a plane crash. Statistically speaking, it's nearly impossible. So I decided to fake my death.

All I did was build a small plane in my head and then crash it into the ground with a single question: "If I died today, what would I regret not being able to do?"

You'd think it would take more than that, but pretend planes are surprisingly easy to destroy.

I thought about the question at hand for a few minutes, and then I wrote this down in my Five Star college-ruled notebook (wide ruled is for lazy people).

If I died today,

1. I wouldn't get to write a book.
2. I wouldn't get to love my wife.
3. I wouldn't get to play with my kids.

The order of that list should assure you that I am being honest. I put "write a book" above "love my wife" and "play with my kids." I bronze medaled my own children. What a jerk. And as a Christian, I should have at least given God a cameo on that list. At the bare minimum, I should have said, "4. I wouldn't get to worship God." But in my defense, if I'm dead then I'm in heaven with God, so maybe I'm in the clear on that one.

Regardless of the complete lack of nobleness in my list, I had one. And I stared at it for a minute and thought, *That really didn't do a whole lot for me. I bet capers will taste the same this afternoon, and tomorrow I won't notice the way fresh morning dew hangs on lilac bushes.*

So I asked myself another question: "Are those the things I'm spending time doing right now?"

Stomach punch.

Suddenly what was a fun list of dreams for the future started to haunt me. If those were the three things that mattered to me most, why wasn't I spending much time pursuing them? What was I waiting for? If they were important, why wasn't I really doing any of them?

That day, I decided to change my life. I wrote a book. I took my wife out to a candlelight dinner at a restaurant that puts the prices on the menu in cursive. And I built a tree house with my kids that had a trap door and a tire swing. Whole thing took about four hours.

That's not what I did. I'd like to edit my history and tell you that those two questions became my driving motivation and, from that moment on, my entire life was different. It wasn't. The land of Learning doesn't offer escape pods to the land of Mastering.

Instead, I felt like I had received an invitation to be more awesome more often. I wasn't going to wait for a bout with cancer or a real plane crash to teach me that life is fleeting. I didn't need to see everything flash before my eyes to know that it would some day.

I'd received a postcard from awesome, and it had two questions on it:

1. If I died today, what would I regret not being able to do?
2. Are those the things I'm spending time doing right now?

And the choice to answer those questions was mine. I could ignore them and wake up at 75 and regret my life, suddenly caught off guard that it's almost over. Or I could wrestle with those questions and admit a few things:

I was scared to write a book. Talking about it was easier and safer than trying it and possibly finding out I didn't have what it takes. I had clutched apathy tightly like a shield to my chest for years, pretending I didn't really care about writing a book.

I was also lazy.

I was content to be an average husband and an average dad.

Those weren't fun things to admit about myself, but they did bring about a certain amount of clarity. If I didn't change something, the years were going to stack themselves on top of each other until I didn't have any left. That's what happens to most people at the end of their lives and what Bronnie Ware discovered in her patients.

She's a nurse in Australia who spent years caring for people in the last weeks of their lives. She wrote a book called *The Top Five Regrets of the Dying*.

The number-one regret? "I wish I'd had the courage to live a life true to myself, not the life others expected of me."

"This was the most common regret of all," explains Ware. "When people realize that their life is almost over and look back clearly on it, it is easy to see how many dreams have gone unfulfilled. Most people had not honored even half of their dreams and had to die knowing that it was due to choices they had made, or not made. Health brings a freedom very few realize, until they no longer have it."[3]

For the average person, the reality of death is the only thing more powerful than the fear of living the life you truly desire. But this isn't a book about being average. It's a book about being awesome.

I'm not sure how you'd answer those two previous questions, but I know if you're going to be more awesome more often, you need to. And preferably long before you ever need a nurse like Bronnie Ware.

Climb in your own plane and crash it today. There's plenty of open ground in the land of Learning for another smoldering wreckage.

## THE GINGERBREAD TRAIL

Did you come up with a perfect answer to the plane crash questions? It only took me about fifteen minutes. I got a smoothie afterward. Pretty enjoyable afternoon, actually. Must be something wrong with you.

That's what we think when we start learning ways to be more awesome more often. We think it should be easy work, and when it's not, we want to give up. The truth is, learning about who we are is rarely easy.

This path may feel new at first. Traversing through the land of Learning may feel like a maiden voyage. But the funny thing is that you've hidden yourself clues along this road forever.

The clues were about what you really loved doing. They didn't all make it this far into your life, but more than you can imagine remain strewn throughout the land of Learning. The clues are the gingerbread trail leading to your definition of awesome.

If you've recovered from the pretend trauma and the real disappointment of not riding that yellow inflatable slide, it's time to look for a few hints. Especially since they can come from the strangest places, or so I learned with my mother-in-law.

When my blog took off and I started really leaning into my dream, people would always ask her, "How does he do it all?"

Her answer to her friends was perfect: "That's the wrong question to ask. The real question is, 'How did he *not* do it before?'"

Where were the thousands of words that were now going to social media and book-writing going before I started working on my dream?

They weren't new. I didn't turn into someone completely different at age 30. I'd always had those ideas inside me and now that they had a home, my mother-in-law had to wonder, where did they live before?

The answer is Post-it notes. And the backs of envelopes, and scrap pieces of paper.

I was writing tweets ten years before Twitter was launched. I would scribble down short thoughts like, "I wish I knew more unhappy rich people," and then leave them on the kitchen counter. A week later my wife would throw them all away 'cause they looked like a pile of garbage. And then I would tell her she just threw away the great American novel. It was a pretty fun cycle we had going.

I didn't know it at the time, but my desire to share ideas, to write books, to help people had been trying to break through the surface of my days for years. It had been sending up flares from deep within my heart, trying to get my attention for decades.

But I missed it. And I don't want the same thing to happen to you.

If you had a hard time answering the plane crash question, let's approach the idea of awesome from a slightly different angle.

Instead of asking, "What would I love to start doing?" let's ask, "What can I not stop doing?"

What's something in your life that you keep coming back to? For me, it was writing ideas. Try as I might, I couldn't stop leaving notes around the house, writing friends long-winded emails with scattered ideas in them, or dominating dinner parties by cornering friends to hear my thoughts. It was a compulsion.

What's something you can't stop doing? Chances are there's some passion or dream or activity that's survived for years. You don't respect it; we never do. My friend Chris, who is in his late 30s, told me one night, "I just don't know what any of my passions are." That would have been troubling if he hadn't just shown me the antique railroad car he had spent months rebuilding and reconditioning by hand. What was once a forgotten piece of wood and metal on a trash heap had been lovingly, painstakingly crafted into a conversation-stopping centerpiece in his living room. But he wasn't sure what his passions were. We're horrible at seeing the potential of our own dreams.

They are there. Hiding out in the shadows of our days, waiting for us to admit they matter. Waiting for us to see that a pile of notes could be a book, or a continued love of volunteering at a local animal shelter could be a business, or a compulsion to attend the Mumford & Sons concert three nights in a row could be the start of something bigger.

What can you not stop doing?

## BE A STUDENT OF YOU

One afternoon I had lunch at Mellow Mushroom with a pastor. He wanted to write a book and didn't know where to start. He asked me, "Should I take three months off to write it? Take a sabbatical, get a cabin somewhere, and hole up in there until it's done? Or should I take the opposite route? Write a page a day so that by the end of the year I have over 300 pages done?"

He continued to rattle off options based on a number of different books about writing.

Finally, I asked him, "How old are you?"

"Forty-two," he replied.

"Then you've got forty-two years of research. You've got forty-two years of evidence indicating how you best accomplish things. You need to be a student of you. What do you do best?" I asked.

"Well, I love sharing stories in my sermons. I'm a storyteller. That's my favorite thing to do, and for the last twelve years, that's what I've been doing every Sunday morning when I preach."

"Well then, get your sermons transcribed. You can have someone transcribe them for $3 an hour. You've probably already got a great start down the path of writing a book."

He was flabbergasted at how smart I am. Or maybe at how obvious that solution was. No one ever thinks that one element of his or her life can inform another. We think we have to start from scratch each time. But we don't.

You need to be a student of you. Don't walk down this road to awesome as if you've never been awesome before. You have. You've succeeded at something. Something came naturally. Something worked. How can you apply that to this?

If you were able to stick to a diet for six months, how did you do it? What about that experience overlaps with your new road to awesome? If you've had success at work, even if you don't love your job, what are the things you can learn from that experience? What skills came out shining?

We usually don't take enough time to study ourselves. Subsequently, we learn the same things over and over again. Or worse than that, we discount everything we've learned for the latest technique espoused in a book.

That's one of the greatest presumptions of many business and self-help books. They tend to have a one-size-fits-all approach. There's often that section or specific chapter about goal setting that involves an incredibly complicated, detailed list and a system of checks and balances that exceeds that of the US Treasury. Of course the approach worked perfectly for the author, because she's an incredibly detailed, organized person. But maybe that's the absolute worst approach for you. Maybe you're a painter, not a mathematician. But because the book says, "In order to set goals, you have to set them this way," you give it a try. Everything about your previous thirty years on the planet indicates that you will not do well with a complicated checklist approach, but the book says this is the only way.

You try it for a day or a week or a month, and it doesn't take. You then assume you're lousy at goal setting and quit.

But maybe you're a bird reading a book about how to be a fish. You can discipline yourself all you want, gather as much will-power as is available to you, but it's not going to matter. You've got wings, not fins.

The solution to this problem is to share principles that are true of everyone and applications that are flexible. As we continue to march down the road to awesome, that's what we're going to do. The five stages, for instance, are true for everyone. The road to awesome always travels through them.

However, the method you use to travel from one destination to the next will be determined by your own experience— what you're made of, what you desire, and what you've done to this point.

Measure each action we discuss against what you know to be true of yourself. Be a student of you, and then choose your own means of travel through these stages. I can only describe their existence and offer suggestions on traversing them that have worked for me and other travelers I've met along the way. The point is not that you copy exactly what I've done.

The point is that you take the principles, customize them to what you know of yourself, and keep moving through the lands.

Do this and you will be able to make progress. Continue doing this, and you will reach your version of awesome many times in your lifetime.

* * *

My first Christmas as a husband I decided to make my wife some furniture.

I'd never learned woodworking. I'd never been taught furniture making. I'm pretty sure I got a B-minus in shop class in the seventh grade (although I think the issue was that my wooden key caddy was over-shellacked).

Nothing about my previous twenty-four years on the planet would indicate that I would be amazing at building something with my bare hands. But I was in the land of Learning, and when you're there, you try new things. You take new risks. You explore new passions.

Emboldened with courage, I found a nightstand in a Restoration Hardware catalog. I ripped out the page and went to our local Home Depot. I purchased a jigsaw, 'cause those things seemed interesting, a handsaw, a huge box of nails, and a few pieces of wood.

Realizing that wasn't enough for a first Christmas gift, I also bought a woodcarving kit. Our wedding invitations had a silhouette of a topiary on them, and my plan was to carve that same design into the door of the nightstand I lovingly crafted.

Tools in hand, I retreated to the dark basement of our 1920s rental house in Arlington, Massachusetts.

For days I worked, so excited to show my wife how much I loved her. So giddy about discovering this new passion. So eager for our grandkids to one day say, "Grandpa Awesome-Jon, tell us the nightstand story again. Tell us!"

Finally, after many a night of sweat and sawdust, I asked my wife to come downstairs. I couldn't wait for Christmas. The excitement was too much! She came down the basement stairs, and I took her by the hand.

With the flourish of a magician who insists you call him an illusionist, I revealed to her what I had built and ultimately learned: "I suck at woodworking."

There, next to our washing machine, was the world's ugliest box. It weighed roughly fourteen pounds and had approximately thirty-seven crooked nails protruding out of it from all angles.

It didn't look like a Restoration Hardware nightstand.

We laughed for a few minutes. I may have been crying. Then my dad put me in touch with an elderly friend of his who built furniture. He agreed to build the nightstand if I would be his assistant and supply the wood. So one night in early December I packed up all the lumber I had purchased and headed to his shop.

After I unloaded it, he eyeballed it for approximately three seconds and said, "Were you making a boomerang? This is the most warped wood I've ever seen in my life. I can't believe they actually sold you this. Put it back in the car; we'll use something else."

I tried to assist by holding down planks or handing him tools. But about fifteen minutes in, he stopped, turned off the machine he was using, and invited me to go home.

Apparently I wasn't even qualified to hold lumber. I got the heave-ho from the old man because my very presence was making things difficult. He was very kind about it. He told me, "You go home. I'll build it for you and call you when it is done."

To this day it sits in our living room, a constant testament not to failure but to the land of Learning.

The way you pass through the land of Learning is that you try a bunch of things. Fear would love for you to try just one, get discouraged, and then march right back to average.

But you won't. You need to get a jigsaw, some warped wood, and a bunch of nails and head into the shop. You need to tinker and build and break and put back together. It may not look awesome at first. Maybe woodworking isn't your particular brand of awesome. It wasn't mine. Neither was painting. But I didn't know the truth about either until I tried. And learned.

Your path through Learning may be littered with sawdust and chunks of warped wood with dozens of bent nails sticking out of them. And that's expected. Give yourself the freedom to make some really ugly furniture.

That's what Learning is all about. I first saw it in my dad.

He's an adventurous guy. In the 1980s, he started a Southern Baptist Church in Massachusetts, something that was unheard-of at the time.

He had three kids, a young wife, and a pretty decent mustache. But other than that, he didn't have a whole lot when he moved our family to Ipswich, Massachusetts. After seminary

and working at a church, he decided to plant Grace Baptist in Marlboro.

Decades later, when I talked to him about that experience, he laughed with me and shared how he's always looked at doing new things. Often when you strike out on a new adventure like the dozens you're exploring in the land of Learning, people will ask you, "Have you ever done that before?" The particulars of the "that" are immaterial. It could be starting a business, going to college, or traveling around the world. And here is how my dad (and now I) answer when life asks us the question, "Have you ever done that before?"

"No, but I'm about to."

Have you ever been on national television? No, but I'm about to.

Have you ever written a book of poems before? No, but I'm about to.

Have you ever biked across the country for charity? No, but I'm about to.

You say that simple phrase, and then you do it. That's it. That's all it takes to beat back that monster called "my first time."

Do it once and then twice and then thrice and then ten times, until before you know it, you're out of the land of Learning.

Every journey has a first step. Every dream has a first destination.

The land of Learning is yours. And now it's about time to move on to your next destination.

## THE LAST STOP IN THE LAND OF LEARNING

I'm almost positive there's not a chapter in *What to Expect When You're Expecting* that talks about what to do if your 1-year-old eats a cigarette butt.

That's what happened to my friends one night while they were waiting for a table at a Mexican restaurant. Sophie, their incredibly fast toddler, was crawling around on the sidewalk in front of the restaurant and made her move before anyone could stop her. For the next day, her adorable little baby breath smelled like Pall Malls. I don't fault my friends; it's hard to raise babies.

For the first three years you have a kid, you're not really parenting. You're protecting. Your job is to basically keep them from hurting themselves with tables and cabinets and toilets and dogs and cats and knives and anything within their surprisingly long wingspan. Which is why baby earrings have never made sense to me.

Why would I attach a shiny, sharp, windpipe-sized object to my child's head? I have Fort Knox–style drawer locks that make getting a fork out a Criss Angel magic trick. Why would I make sure my baby is always traveling with tiny little weapons inches from her mouth? Why not just dangle a live scorpion from her pacifier? Just to kind of see what happens?

The only thing that makes even less sense than earrings for babies is Bunsen burners for seventh graders. "I've got an idea! Let's give the most awkward, emotionally charged, hormone-intoxicated humans on the planet access to a flame and a never-ending gas source. The guys are all trying to show off in front of the girls; the girls are distracted wondering if the guys are even noticing them; they've all grown long arms and legs they barely know how to use. What better time in life to introduce them to the wonder that is the Bunsen burner? What could possibly go wrong?"

But it happens. In the seventh grade you go from building crooked coat-hanger models of the solar system to having ready access to the sun's source of heat in the science lab.

Which, as it happens, is also your last stop in the land of Learning.

It's the last building on the road. On a hook by the door hangs a lab jacket and a pair of safety goggles. (That word is impossible to spell correctly once you've typed "Google" a million times.)

As you put them on and walk down the hall, you'll find yourself in a simple laboratory. There are beakers and colorful liquids, tubes and pipes and jars. If you lost your science notebook in the seventh grade and almost flunked the class because Mrs. Murtaugh did not play around when it came time to deliver your semester-long science notebook, hypothetically speaking, you may be a little nervous.

But don't be. There's only one thing you have to do in this laboratory.

Experiment.

That's it. That's the action you have to embrace in the land of Learning. Because scientists don't fail; they experiment. They blow things up. They burn things down. They tinker. They smash. They mix. And when an experiment doesn't go the right way, they don't call it a failure. They say, "Look what we learned. We thought it would go one way and it went the opposite! What can we take away from this that will help us with our next experiment?" That's why James Dyson had 5,126 prototypes before completing his industry-changing vacuum cleaner. It's why Angry Birds, the wildly popular app, was

Rovio's fifty-second attempt at a game. It's why WD-40 had thirty-nine other formulas that came before it. Everyone who succeeds learns through experimentation.[4]

No matter what fear and doubt tell you, your identity is not at stake with the decisions you make and the actions you take as you learn. You're a son or a daughter. You're a father or a mother. You're a husband or a wife. The Bunsen burner won't change that. You were you before you walked in the building. You'll be you when you walk out. Only more awesome.

So fire it up. It's time to blow some things up and see what the debris can ultimately teach you about yourself and your truest dreams.

# 5

# EDITING

**HOW WILL YOU KNOW** when you've entered the land of Editing?

You won't.

Moving on.

Wait, that can't be right.

We want steps. We want a checklist with fourteen boxes we can check off so we know we're perfectly prepared for what's next.

You can't have them. I can't either. The map doesn't work that way. And neither does life.

That's like asking, "When do you become a man?" I really hope it's not when you learn how to make furniture by hand. In the movie *Red Dawn*, it was when Thomas C. Howell shot a deer and drank its blood. Or in the remake when Zac Effron shot a unicorn and stole its tail (I haven't seen the remake, but I'm assuming that happens).

The problem with trying to draw up really precise boundaries is that there's too much overlap between the stages. They bleed into each other more like the colors of a real rainbow and less like the colors on a paint wheel at a hardware store.

Just when you think you're out of one stage, you'll find yourself stepping back into the previous one, and vice versa. For instance, I hope even when you're in the land of Guiding, you won't stop learning about your specific version of awesome. I hope if you have the chance to help someone else while you're in the land of Learning you won't say, "I'd love to lend you a hand, but I haven't crossed into Guiding yet, sooooo . . ."

The easiest way to tell you're in the land of Editing and no longer in Learning is with a math metaphor.

Learning is about addition. Editing is about subtraction.

In the land of Editing, you're going to take the fifteen or fifteen hundred things you learned and see which ones seem to stick to you. What passions, dreams, hopes, and callings will you be carrying deeper into this journey with you? Which will you leave on the side of the road for someone else to pick up? They are not broken or ruined; they are simply not for us. They are part of someone else's unique definition of awesome.

Editing is the phase of your journey where Michelangelo stands in front of the meticulously selected block of marble. Out of an entire quarry, this is the one he has chosen. And now, with a chisel and a hammer he will remove the pieces that do not belong so that David is finally revealed.

## CUE THE FOG

My friend Tim in Atlanta often misses breakfast meetings.

He doesn't want to. He is actually one of the kindest, most conscientious people I've ever met. He sends handwritten thank-you notes after he eats dinner at our house, the kind of notes that my wife holds up and says, "See? See? This is how to be a gentleman."

But he has a hard time getting to breakfast on time or at all.

One morning it was because his iPhone battery was dead and its alarm didn't go off.

Another morning it was because his iPhone was in another room and he didn't hear it.

Another morning it was because he had the sound turned down too low and he didn't hear it.

And still another morning it was because . . . well, you get the picture.

The solution to this dilemma is not very difficult. It is not complex. One must not call a brainstorming meeting to hash out possible fixes.

The solution is a $10 alarm clock.

It couldn't be simpler. It automatically fixes all the issues he's had with his iPhone alarm. So why didn't Tim just fix the problem with that simple solution the first time his iPhone clock plan failed?

Because we love complex problems and are terrified of simple solutions.

We tend to add complexities to our challenges because if the problem is simple to solve, then we have to change. And change is scary. So when faced with a challenge we really don't want to fix, we tend to overcomplicate the issues. We blame our iPhones for not waking us up. What did we even do before we had cell phones with alarm clocks?

That's the great temptation with the Editing stage. When we're there, we get a little skittish and fire up the fog machine. Rather than edit our lives, i.e., start to make decisions, we cloud our path and pretend there's a fog of complexity in the way. How can we possibly be expected to make any progress in this type of weather? It'd be dangerous to even go out on a night like this. Maybe this whole awesome thing was a mistake and we should head back to the familiar road of average.

And so we retreat, back to what we've always known. There is a suffocating comfort to it all. Letting go is not easy. The hoarders we see on TV who are stockpiling cats and newspapers have nothing on us emotional hoarders. At least the things they refuse to give up create physical piles before their eyes. They stink and cause a scene that can't be ignored.

On the other hand, the dreams you've always had but refuse to actually work on tend to create hidden piles you don't have to look at unless you really force yourself to. The hopes you refuse to edit and learn to master don't rot so tangibly—at least at first. You can skate through decades without a family member knowing, but then one day you'll run into me on a flight to Baltimore just like the woman we talked about in the first chapter.

That night we met, she was essentially asking me the same thing I had asked myself at the kindergarten in Vietnam. *How did I get here?* How did I get to 72 with so few of my dreams ever acted on?

How did I get here?

You will say those five words in your life. Everyone will. In the middle of a bad relationship or a career you feel is stealing years of your life, you will say, "How did I get here?"

The first time local media interviews you about your wildly successful business or someone wants you to sign the book you wrote, you will say, "How did I get here!"

And the only difference will be the punctuation.

If you choose to be awesome, you'll aim for a whole lot more exclamation points and a whole lot fewer question marks. Because it's not a question of whether you'll say those five words. It's a question of *how* you'll say those five words.

Will you be making a declaration like a thunderstruck blogger in the mountains of Vietnam?

Will you be asking a question like a retiree flying over Baltimore and decades of life?

I can't find the woman I sat next to on that flight. The Internet still has its limits, but if I could, I now know how I would answer her question. I would tell her the same thing I'd tell you.

Start today, regardless of your age. Turn off the fog machine. Acting on the dreams you learned about in your previous destination is not complicated. Walking deeper into the land of Editing is not as complex as fear and doubt are trying to tell you it is. In fact, it starts with just one question.

## THE BIGGEST QUESTION YOU CAN ASK

One morning some bakery owners asked me to help them figure out their path to awesome.

They didn't have big, floppy baker hats on or any artisanal breads with them, which was disappointing, but I got over it. They stopped me in the hall of a hotel at a business event. They were married and told me their story:

"We're sick of Texas. We want seasons again. And hills and trees. We've got a little bakery in town that people love. We make different breads and sandwiches. It's growing and we've started to build up a local following. But now we want to move to Idaho. And we don't know what we should do when we get there. Should we open another bakery? Should we focus on wholesale? Should we do catering? Should we have a little restaurant?"

As we talked, it became clear that they had gone through a long list of questions as they journeyed through the land of Editing:

What would make the most money?

What did the town in Idaho need?

What type of business could they grow the fastest?

What type of business would have the lowest overhead?

Which idea would take the least amount of equipment?

They had run through a laundry list of questions but had failed to ask the most important question there is in the land of Editing. So there in the hall, I said to them, "Well, what gives you the most joy?"

You would have thought I'd thrown a cat at them. For weeks they'd been debating the move to Idaho. They'd worked hard on the challenge of moving. They'd studied and debated. They were attending an exclusive business event for high-performing entrepreneurs when I met them. They'd looked at the problem from every possible angle, except one: joy.

Most of us never get there. We never ask the question, "What gives me the most joy?"

I think some of us feel guilty even saying those words out loud. As if perhaps it's a selfish thing to think, *What gives me joy?* As if perhaps joy is acceptable for rare moments on the weekend or surprising glimpses of sunsets while on vacation, but it has no real purpose in the real world. It would be selfish to think we could have more joy. (The truth is that real life-change and the joy of being who you are designed to be always results in self-lessness, not selfishness.)

Some of my Christian friends would push back at this idea as a matter of principle. We've been so overwhelmed with the prosperity gospel, or "name it and claim it," that we've swung the pendulum the other direction and think that perhaps the only way to serve God is to make sure we're miserable. In the prodigal son parable, a young son demands his inheritance from his father, spends it all in wild living, and then returns home expecting to be turned into a servant by his greatly disappointed father. Instead, he is thrown a wild, lavish, joyful party. Some Christians in that moment would have refused the party, saying, "No, no, this is too much. Is there somewhere I can serve on the farm instead? A foot-washing station perhaps? This party is giving me way too much joy."

But whether or not you're a Christian, the point is we have an uncomfortable relationship with joy when it comes to figuring out our lives.

So instead of asking, "What gives me the most joy?" we ask easier questions, like, "What will make me the most money?" That's not a bad question. It's a great question to ask eventually; I have no issue with making money. I wrote this book on a laptop I bought with money. I am a fan of money.

But money isn't a calling. It's a consequence.

That's the problem; most of us ask results questions.

What will make money?

What jobs are available in the market right now?

What industry is growing?

What do I have the most experience doing?

Those are great questions, but they're not the right questions to ask first, because they don't reveal your awesome.

There are a million things that will make you money but leave you miserable. That's not awesome.

Your diploma may say "Merchant Marine" and your greatest joy says "Counselor."

If steel mills are hiring in your town and the job market is tough, that doesn't mean steel is your awesome.

You may have spent thirty years being a pastor, and your awesome still says, "Let's be a beekeeper too."

Those aren't fictional examples. Those are real people I know who all dared to ask that question, "What gives me the most joy?"

I dare you to ask it too.

## DON'T BUILD PARK BENCHES IF YOU LOVE FRISBEE

Usually when you come across two men in the woods with a hammer, it's a cause for concern, especially if your hands aren't weapons like mine. But that Saturday afternoon my dad and I didn't stumble across something dangerous—we stumbled across something awesome.

There, in a small clearing of a large park near our house in Atlanta, were another father and son. The father, who I think had a beard, because I add beards to a lot of people in my memories, was holding a long signpost. His teenage son stood above him, slowly hammering the post into a hole they had dug in the hard soil.

Turns out they weren't burying a body—but thanks for that automatic assumption, CBS—they were building signs for the Frisbee golf course. The holes were scattered about the park and hard to find if you didn't know the course well. So one by one, hole by hole, this dynamic duo was marking the way with eighteen different signs.

The father looked up as we walked upon them. Without letting go of the post, he explained, "My son is getting his Eagle Scout badge. This sure beats building another park bench." Then he grinned a big (bearded?) smile and got back to work.

I'm not an Eagle Scout, but I remember growing up with a kid who was. I remember my mom kind of pitching me the idea by telling me about the project that had pushed him over the edge and sealed the deal with the Eagle Scout badge committee. Guess what he did?

He cleaned and repainted the fire hydrants in my town. Now, it's possible that he had a deep passion for fire hydrants. Maybe his daddy was a fire hydrant man. His daddy's daddy was a fire hydrant man. Hydrants were in his blood. But chances are good that he didn't love them.

Chances are, he thought earning the honor of being an Eagle Scout meant doing something awful. He had to be a martyr and do the thing no "regular" boy would do.

As you edit your life and search through the things you're passionate about, don't build a park bench if you secretly love Frisbee. Don't buy the lie that changing the world has to be a chore or make you miserable. Be brave enough to have fun with whatever you whittle down in your life.

## AWESOME ISN'T A JOB TITLE

One day at a conference in Oklahoma a gentleman tried to stump me during a Q&A session. From the back of the room, his hand shot up and he asked, "If everyone finds their dream job, who is going to pick up my trash?"

I would have swept his leg Cobra Kai style, but he was old and even from the stage I could tell that his bones were brittle. So instead, I stammered some ridiculous answer, knowing full well that I would come up with the perfect response a few hours later as I was driving alone to the airport. And I did. Here it is:

"You're confusing awesome with a job title. Awesome is the core of who you are. It's your heart, your soul, the fabric of what makes you. A job title is just a consequence of you living out of your awesome. I'm not trying to tell people to go out and find new job titles; I'm telling them to escape average."

Then, at that point, if they hadn't wrestled the mic away from me because my sweatiness was indicating an imminent rant, here's how I would have continued:

I once had to call the Apple support desk because the Cloud wrecked my iTunes account. I got stuck in the stratosphere and consequently lost all the music I had purchased over the last ten years. So I called them up and had to spend an hour on the phone with the customer service representative.

While we waited for her to receive information from another department, we started to talk. I asked her, "Is your job hard? I've sat beside customer service departments at jobs I've had, and it seems like it is."

That was a pretty safe assumption on my part. Her job seemed a little miserable to me. Every phone call she received was from someone who was unhappy. Her phone never rang with people telling her thank you or "I love my new laptop! It's working great! I just wanted to let you know!"

People only called when their phone was broken or their hard drive had crashed or the battery in their laptop had overheated and started a small lap fire. (Or when, hypothetically speaking of course, they had spilled coffee inside their laptop and were hoping there was some sort of keyboard shortcut they could press that would open the laptop's bilge pump. Control + Alt + 3, maybe?)

Think of the worst phone call you got at work last week and then multiply that by forty hours, and you've got a clear sense of her job. Or at least I thought that was what she would say. I was wrong.

"I love my job!" she said.

"Really?" I replied. "How so?"

"Well, there are two things I love: learning new things and helping people. And I get to do that all day!" She lit up as she continued to talk about her job.

"Every day I get to help people solve their problems. It's so fun. And I get to learn new things. The technology is changing so fast that every day is different, and I get to learn all about that."

I hung up the phone that day realizing that I had been looking at awesome within the context of a specific application.

That girl's awesome was to help people and learn new things. And once she learned that, once she found that out, she could apply it in a million different ways. She could take a job that a lot of people would say, "It must be hard to do that" and have great joy in it. She had walked through Editing and, instead of digging for a specific job title, she uncovered two joys—learning new things and helping people. Then she looked for ways to apply those more each day.

She understood that being awesome is about finding the core of who you are and what lights you up. Once you've discovered that, you can have a million different jobs.

Take me, for instance, since I'm the only one writing this book right now. Once I edited my life and realized that what I really cared about was sharing ideas, suddenly there were a million dream jobs available. I could become a blogger, an author, a podcast host, a public speaker, a radio show host, a counselor, a consultant, or a copywriter.

The world of dream jobs opened up when I got to the core of what I love to do—when I chiseled away that chunk of marble I found in the land of Learning and discovered the David statue inside of me. Once I found that, my job was just another way I could apply my discovery.

Most of us get it backward. We never take the time to walk through the land of Editing. Instead, we spend a little time in Learning and then say, "Now I need to find the perfect job." But we rarely know what we love doing at that stage, so it's impossible to find the right job. We usually end up frustrated and resolve to let work just pay the bills.

My current job title is "insight architect." I admit, that's a little pretentious sounding. Even typing it kind of made me think, *I wonder if that guy is a jerk?* (The answer is yes, but we'll cover that later in the book.) But can you imagine if, upon leaving the land of Learning, I said, "Instead of finding the awesome inside me, I'm just going to search for a company hiring insight architects. How hard can that be? Country has to be crawling with open positions for that."

Don't just search for a job title. Search for awesome. Once you figure that out, you can be a customer call center representative and still be awesome.

## BLOW UP YOUR SCOREBOARDS

Sometimes people will tell me, "You say everyone can find their dream and be awesome. What if my dream is to win a Grammy, but I'm horrible at singing? What then?"

That's a good challenge and the type of thing that people often throw in the face of those who say, "You can be anything you want to be." If I suck at singing, how can you say I'll win a Grammy?

The short answer is autotune.

The longer, more honest answer is you probably won't.

You can't be "anything you want," but you can be something even better: the best version of you. That's always more enjoyable than trying to force yourself to be something you weren't designed to be (please refer to my dreams of being in the NBA). You want to win a Grammy even though you have no musical ability? That probably isn't going to happen. But that's okay because winning a Grammy isn't your awesome. It's not anyone's. It's just a result on a scoreboard.

So, what if your awesome is to sing? What if your awesome is to express the natural singing talent you have inside you, that bubbling, passionate talent you've kept quiet for so many years? What if you don't need the Grammys to validate your dream?

What if the real definition of awesome is as simple as "singing more today than I did yesterday"?

That may sound silly, but I assure you it's powerful.

With that definition, you get to succeed every time you sing. You get to succeed every time you open your mouth and your heart and let out that talent that is dying to see the light of day.

You get to be Seryn.

They're a band from Denton, Texas. They kind of remind me of Mumford & Sons with more instruments and fewer British accents. Each member plays approximately thirty-seven instruments, and they constantly switch them out in the middle of songs.

I first saw them play at a conference in front of 13,000 people. I was blown away by the energy they filled that arena with that day. Their passion was unbridled, as if they couldn't believe they got to play music in front of people.

I wrote about them on Facebook. A few days later a guy named Larry in the town next to ours emailed me. He said, "I saw you liked that band Seryn. They're playing a house show in my living room. Do you and your wife want to come see them?" We did.

An hour after we arrived, Seryn arrived from New York and set up all the aforementioned instruments in Larry's living room. They tuned everything, had a sip of water, and then launched into their set.

If awesome were measured on a scale of 1 to 10, I expected they'd play at a three or a four, whatever the appropriate level of music is for a corner of taupe carpet next to a loveseat. I was wrong.

The same joy that dominated the stage before 13,000 people was on display in a room full of eighty friends. It was like Seryn couldn't help but play that way. That was what was inside their hearts. In that moment, I learned a simple lesson about being awesome: always play to the size of your heart, not to the size of your audience.

Awesome doesn't let the crowd determine the size of the performance. Awesome gets up for two people or 200. Awesome writes great books even if no one is going to read them. Awesome sweeps the parts of store floors that no foot will ever touch.

Awesome can't help itself.

Awesome has a huge heart. And that's what it always plays to.

The size of the crowd doesn't matter.

The applause of the audience doesn't matter.

The money you make singing doesn't matter.

Don't get me wrong; I hope you get all those things. I hope you have huge audiences and screaming fans and more money than Scrooge McDuck in his money bin. But more than that, I hope if your definition of awesome is to sing, you do it often. And you realize along the way that singing often is what really matters.

If you live your life that way, the results become gravy instead of the missing ingredient to your joy. If you can grab hold of this concept, you can start living an awesome life right this second. You don't need the Grammys to validate your version of awesome. Even if someday they do. That happened to my friend Dave Barnes. He wrote a song that got nominated for a Grammy, and we were all excited for him. But what was even more amazing was that for a decade he'd been making the music he wanted to make every day. The Grammy nomination was a delightful consequence of the awesome life he'd been living, not a validation of it. There's a world of difference, whether you're a musician, a mom, a business owner, or all three.

## THE DIAMOND MINE

Though this book doesn't offer any get-rich-quick schemes, there is a diamond mine on the road to awesome that you need to visit as you pass through the land of Editing.

Have you ever been gem mining?

It's exactly like it sounds, only the gems aren't really gems, and the mining isn't really mining. It should be more aptly titled "gravel bathing," but chances are that mountain tourists wouldn't be interested in that activity.

Here's how it works:

On the side of the road in a small mountain community like Boone, North Carolina, you buy a bucket of gravel and dirt from a "gem mine." You then pour the gravel and dirt into a small container and hold it under a thin stream of water that runs through a trough. As you wash off the mud, you start to see gems like amethyst and fool's gold. You pluck out the best rocks, clean them, and then have one of the gem store owners tell you that you found some amazing ones today, at which point you hot glue them to a picture frame that is now the sharpest, most dangerous item in your house.

Last summer, during our annual trip to see our in-laws, we went gem mining. At the end of the day, we sat at a counter while a geologist told us what each rock meant. He was getting his degree in geology at a local university and actually knew an incredible amount about each stone. He turned them over in his hands carefully, describing each nuance and the forces of nature deep inside the earth that conspired to create them. He'd grab a small flashlight and shine it into a rock to reveal the green hue of an emerald hidden inside. He'd wash crusted dirt off a bit of rock and show the amethyst that was hiding just below the surface.

The rocks were beautiful, with explosions of color and light that seemed to rival that of more expensive stones like rubies and diamonds. But at the end of the day, they were just rocks. So he placed them in an old plastic bag, wrote my daughter's name on the outside with a Sharpie, and handed it back to her.

As we drove home, I started to wonder, *Why do some rocks get to be rocks and some rocks get to be diamonds?*

There are certainly some mechanical characteristics that make diamonds valuable, but their price is nowhere near what they are actually worth. There are actually several gemstones that are far more rare than diamonds.[1] So how come a diamond is a diamond and any other rock is just a rock?

Because somebody decided that's how it works.

A diamond is just a rock we collectively assigned the highest value to. That's why the supply is so carefully guarded and monitored, making a diamond worth a lot of money and another stone worth a spot on a picture frame.

Inside the mine in the land of Editing, you've got to decide what in your life is going to be a diamond and what's going to be a rock.

You get to make that decision. You get to assign value to the things in your life, and the value you assign will radically change how you interact with them.

Scientists call this "value attribution." The value we place on things is a powerful, powerful force. In some ways it guides our perception of the entire planet. The *Washington Post* proved this once with a well-known story about a violinist and a subway.

One morning, in the middle of rush hour, they placed Joshua Bell, one of the world's greatest violinists, on a subway platform, dressed in casual clothes. Into his skilled hands they placed a $3.5 million violin designed by Antonio Stradivari in 1713. He then proceeded to play the most complicated, amazing arrangements of music. Can you imagine how many people paused during their commute to take in a concert that would normally cost hundreds of dollars in one of the world's greatest concert halls? The answer is seven.

More than 1,000 people passed Bell as he played, and only seven people stopped to listen.[2]

Only seven people stopped for a minute to give the moment the gravity it certainly deserved. The thousand other people who walked by? As the authors of the book *Sway* suggest, they had already assigned value to that subway performer. The sound of the beautiful music wafting through the air couldn't change that. The design of the multimillion-dollar violin couldn't break through that. The speed and undeniable skill the violinist's hands demonstrated couldn't break through either.

"As they passed by Bell," write Ori and Rom Brafman, "most subway riders didn't even glance in his direction. Instead of hearing an outstanding concert, they heard street music."[3] They had decided the subway was full of rocks, and the appearance of one of the world's greatest diamonds wasn't going to change that.

I didn't particularly like the implications value attribution had in my own life. It was fun to say, "My kids are a top priority to me, my wife is a top priority to me, what I write is a top priority to me," but sometimes I found myself treating them like rocks.

How did I know? Because I wasn't giving them the most valuable currency I own—time.

I was forced to ask myself, *Are my wife and kids and writing getting the best of my time and creativity or the rest of my time and creativity?* Was I calling the right things diamonds and the right things rocks? Or was it possible I had it backward?

That's the goal of our entire time in the land of Editing. We have to, and more importantly *get* to decide what we'll call diamonds and what we'll call rocks. That decision, and our ability to constantly come back to it to make sure we're staying true, has the power to change the way you see the entire world.

The challenge to editing your own value system is that the world will constantly try to convince you that you've got it wrong. When you walk out of the mine holding your diamonds in your hand, the rest of the world may try to convince you they are rocks. Don't listen. You should never chase awesome with someone else's definition.

## FINDING YOUR DIAMONDS

Let's not overcomplicate this.

It's actually really easy to find your diamonds. They're hidden in plain sight right on your calendar. In fact, time is the only honest indication of what really matters to us.

Intentions are ambitious liars. If you ask your intentions what your diamonds are right now, they'll tell you whatever it is you want to hear. Instead, we're going to do a quick interview of your calendar.

In the last twenty-four hours, what did you spend your time doing? In the last week, what received the greatest deposit of your time? Work, probably, but how much did it really get? And where did the rest of your week go?

When I walked out of the diamond mine believing my wife, kids, and writing were my priorities, I had to consult my calendar. What it instantly revealed was that I was spending fifty to sixty hours a week working. It further indicated that my wife and kids were getting almond-thin slivers of my time—something like one-tenth that amount.

My intentions told me what they had always told me: You're such a great husband! You're such a great father!

But my calendar told a different story.

Realizing this, guess what I did at my next job? I worked from 7:00 a.m. to 4:00 p.m. Not everybody did. It wasn't a given. It was something I had to be deliberate about, something I had to protect. But I couldn't ignore my family and treat them like rocks all the while pretending I was treating them like diamonds.

Want to find the rocks and diamonds in your life? Look at your calendar. Don't like what you find? Edit it. You own the calendar. It's your employee. You don't report to it; it reports to you. Edit it down so that diamonds can remain diamonds.

## THE PROBLEM OF MULTIPLE PASSIONS

My friend Matt is a pastor. One day he and his wife wrote a book. It took longer than one day, but that's how fast you assume other writers are able to finish their books.

He was excited about the book releasing but had a bit of a dilemma. Churches across the country were asking him to speak about his book, but he couldn't go because he worked on

Sundays. (My dad was a pastor, and if you're wondering what pastors do the rest of the week, the answer is Frisbee. It's essentially a one-day-a-week profession. Cush.)

Matt asked me if he should take a six-month sabbatical from the church when the book came out so that he could go speak about it. I told him in a rambling way what I thought and then came home.

I shared the challenge with my wife. I described it as a real pickle. Jenny listened for thirty seconds and then solved the dilemma with a single question.

"Is he trying to be a pastor or an author? If his long-term goal is to be an author who writes books and travels around the country speaking at 100 different churches, then he should take the sabbatical. If his goal is to be a pastor of a church, then he shouldn't take the sabbatical. He's already accomplishing his goal. Being away from his own church for six months would be failure."

Dang it, Jenny and your succinct wisdom!

She was right. The answer to Matt's dilemma was pretty simple. What did success look like? If he were to go inside the observatory tower that is along the path through Editing, what would he see in the distance?

If there were two paths in the woods—two passions from which he could choose one to follow—which one ended the way he wanted it to end?

From the observatory tower, which path led to the destination he was most excited about?

Those are the same questions I'd ask you if we were having cinnamon dulce lattes.

If you've got a pile of possibilities in front of you right now and the idea of editing is overwhelming, step up into the observatory tower and gaze into the land of Harvesting. Which destination feels like success?

Which one feels good, but not great?

Which one feels okay, but not awesome?

When I did this exercise, it forced me to realize that to progress as a copywriter in the company I worked for, I would probably need to become a creative director. I would manage projects and people, which would mean I'd spend less time actually writing. That pretty quickly became a destination I wasn't eager to arrive at.

If you've got ten paths, this simple exercise will help you eliminate a few pretty quickly. Especially the ones you're just good at. Just because you're good at something doesn't mean it's the road to awesome for you. You may be an amazing dentist. You are able to fix people's teeth by just gazing at them with your eyes. But if you were honest, if you didn't have the practice, if people didn't constantly tell you how great you are at dentistry, if you hadn't already invested so much of your life down that path, would you admit, "I don't love being a dentist"?

That's what happened to a friend of mine who wrote me this email:

I am 28 years old and recently graduated from dental school. I am currently working as a dentist for a chain of dental offices. This may seem well and good, especially financially, but about halfway through school, I discovered that I really have no passion for the dental profession. I have no hopes and dreams for the future. I don't want my own practice or anything like that. I am not happy practicing dentistry and basically just tolerate each day. Each day seems to get worse as I move along, and given that I've only been doing it for about eight months, I don't know what will happen a few years from now. . . . Basically, I am listless and bored at work. I just feel like I'm drifting and that I'm missing bigger and better opportunities out there. Don't get me wrong, I have a very good job—it pays well and I have good benefits—but I'm not happy at all. I have no intentions of quitting at the time, but I would if I didn't have a massive loan debt from school and a degree that only offers me the luxury of practicing dentistry.

Can you imagine the pressure that guy is feeling? Can you imagine waking up at 28 with $200,000 in student loans and realizing you're in the wrong career? Everything you've worked so hard for, all the decisions you made, all the classes you took, everything you aimed at, brought you to a "How did I get here?" moment—question mark, not exclamation point.

He knew in dental school that the destination on the horizon wasn't where he wanted to end up. Why didn't he stop? Why didn't he quit right then and not become a dentist? The same reason you and I end up in places we never intended to be.

With a thousand small steps.

With a premed class in college. With a loan application one summer. With the first class and second class and third class of dental school. Until one day you wake up and you realize you don't want to be a dentist or a lawyer or an anything. And fear gets loud in that moment. Fear tells you, "It's too late."

It's too late to change now. You've made so many decisions already—it's too late to fix them or change directions.

"It's too late to be a good parent."

"It's too late to go back to school."

"It's too late to start a new profession."

"It's too late to be anything but what you already are."

In those moments, fear and doubt and shame cripple us. We're so frustrated at ourselves that we give up.

We finish the second half of dental school, double our debt, and give fear a few more years of our lives.

I'm not sure what brought you to this moment. I don't know what passions you brought into the observatory and saw through that telescope. I don't know how many obstacles you have in your path. But I do know this. It's not too late.

It's never too late to start.

"It's too late" is a lie that will stay with you if you let it. So don't.

Look through the telescope and see what awesome really looks like for you. Chances are, it's closer and a lot more possible than you think.

Does that mean if we've accrued some bills or amassed some responsibilities that we're going to ignore them and just "go for it"? No. Never. That mind-set is a dream killer. There's nothing awesome about kicking off your dream on a foundation of broken promises and ignored responsibilities.

We're going to pay off our debts.

We're going to edit the unnecessary pieces of marble around us and then hustle in the right direction.

We're going to work harder than we've ever worked as we enter the land of Mastering.

If the telescope reveals a definition of awesome we're not excited about, we're going to leave that dream in the observatory tower, even if that seems very costly.

That's the pressure Bill Watterson, the creator of the *Calvin and Hobbes* comic strip, faced years ago. He had tens of millions of dollars on the table if he'd just license *Calvin and Hobbes* for products. A mug here, a greeting card there, a calendar and a pair of boxer shorts—there was no end to the list of products Bill Watterson could have put his work on. It would have guaranteed him a fortune.

So then why didn't he go the licensing route? I'll let him explain:

As a practical matter, licensing requires a staff of assistants to do the work. The cartoonist must become a factory foreman, delegating responsibilities and overseeing production of things he does not create. Some cartoonists don't mind this, but I went into cartooning to draw cartoons, not to run a corporate empire. If I were to undermine my own characters like this, I would have taken the rare privilege of being paid to express my own ideas and given it up to be an ordinary salesman and a hired illustrator.[4]

Watterson stood in the observatory and saw a harvest he didn't want. Even with millions of dollars on the line, he walked away from the licensing. The joy of cartooning and the magic of the story he got to tell were worth more than becoming a master at something he had never wanted to do. Was Watterson already wealthy from the comic strip? Without a doubt, but if you read any article about him you see a picture of someone who would have drawn cartoons for free because that was his awesome. And when presented with an offer to trade it in for what many would call success, he passed. May we all love whatever it is we do that much.[4]

## STILL TOO MANY PASSIONS?

Hopefully you left a handful of passions in the observatory tower. You like knitting, but running your own knitting store doesn't sound very fun. That one is just going to be a hobby, not your road to awesome.

But chances are, you still have a number of things you think could be awesome. That's okay. I had twenty-six different 1099s in 2010 as I walked through the land of Learning. In addition to my full-time job, I tried my hand at fourteen different freelance writing projects. From video scripts to PowerPoint presentations and everything in between. I experimented in the land of Learning. That's what learning is all about, trying a lot of different things in a lot of different ways.

But we're Editing now, and maybe you don't know which passions matter the most to you. People often tell me that. "I have multiple passions. I don't know which one to start on first." I think that's an awesome problem to have. There are too many things you enjoy in life. Boom! Congratulations. There is a danger with that, though, because people with too many passions tend to do something nobody ever says out loud. Out loud they say, "I have too many passions. I don't know which one to start on first." But what they really mean is, "I have too many passions. So I won't start on any." Then they put their dreams back on the shelf. For another week. Or another month. Or another decade.

If that's you—if you have too many passions and don't know which one to focus on—here's what you do:

Pick one and start.

Don't try to prioritize your list. I used to tell people to do this, and it was a mistake on my part. I would say, "Make a list of all your passions, from most interesting to least interesting. Then start working on the one you are most interested in."

This seemed like good advice, but it's not. What would inevitably happen is that the prioritization lesson would become another point of paralysis. I'd say fifty times, "As you make your list, don't try to make it perfect. Go through it quickly. It doesn't have to be perfect." And then people would take their handful of passions and immediately get stuck trying to come up with a perfect list.

The list is miserable. It's a crippling waste of time. Instead, just pick one and start.

If they're all passions, then what is the worst thing that can happen? You spend time doing something you enjoy and realize along the way it's not what you enjoy the most?

How is that a fail?

That's called an edit. If you wait to create a perfect prioritized list or just simply wait because you don't know where to start, you are guaranteed zero percent joy because you've worked on zero percent of your passions. I'm horrible at math, but even I know some is better than none.

Start on something. Edit it if it's not your awesome. Move on to the next thing.

## THE SEESAW

One day my friend Preston came into my office and said, "Do you want to be a writer who speaks or a speaker who writes?"

At first when he asked me that, it felt like some sort of Buddhist riddle. Like maybe he was going to hit me with a bamboo staff if I didn't answer fast enough. Fortunately he didn't, because it took me six months to understand what he meant.

Was I going to be a writer who writes books and then travels to events to speak about them? Or was I going to be a speaker who writes speeches? If I was going to be a writer, I had to ask myself, *What do writers do?*

This one is going to go quickly so I'll repeat it, but . . . they write. Let me say that again because it's jaw-dropping: they write.

Writers write, right? That's their first priority. They don't book a million speeches throughout the year that prevent them from writing.

They block off their calendars and write.

They research books and write.

They go to writing conferences to hone their craft and write.

Speakers? They do just the opposite.

They book as many speaking engagements as possible and speak.

They work up as many speeches as possible and speak.

They attend speaking conferences to hone their craft and speak.

When I broke it down that simply, it was pretty easy to say yes to some things and no to others.

Most of the time we try to stand in the middle of the passion seesaw and balance perfectly. We're afraid to pick the wrong thing, so we just hover there instead of jumping on one side.

The absurdity is that when I picked writing, it didn't mean I never got to speak. I spoke more times last year than I ever have. I'll speak dozens of times this year and love doing that. I didn't have to decide never to do one of my passions. I just had to decide that there was going to be a winner—the awesome above all awesome. There was going to be a first place if the two passions, writing and speaking, ever went head to head.

And of course they overlap. Most of our passions do. Right now, it's very unlikely your passions are "be a marine biologist, become a Bedouin shepherd, or be a stock trader on Wall Street." Editing your list won't usually prevent you from ever doing your other passions. More often than not, your focus on one passion helps you get even better at another one.

When I focused on being a writer, I got better at writing speeches and presentations. I didn't get rid of the passion to speak. Speaking actually became easier. It just wasn't my final destination on the road to awesome. I wanted to be a writer.

## MOUNTAIN CLIMBER

A one-legged mountain climber once taught me something really interesting.

He'd lost his leg in a climbing accident but still lived on the mountain. In between taking photos for magazines he can be found clinging to cliffs and whatnot.

At an event, I talked to him about the only mountain-climbing story I had. It was a short one that basically went like this:

"Have you seen the cover of the recent *National Geographic*? That guy standing on the cliff? How crazy is that?"

That was all I had. Just like that, I was out of mountain-climbing material.

Fortunately, he had plenty.

"That's Alex Honnold. I'm friends with him. He's amazing."

Alex Honnold is one of the top solo climbers in the world. Solo climbing means he climbs without ropes and without anyone else. The only thing he brings on the mountain is a small bag of chalk and his iPod (probably with the *Quitter* audio book on repeat). He then scales a thousand feet up a cliff, carefully putting his calloused fingers in inch-wide fissures so that he doesn't plummet to his death.

This climber/photographer friend told me that Alex was starting to get a lot of national media attention. One afternoon a team of photographers tied themselves to different parts of the mountain so that they could capture Alex as he ascended. Alex went so fast, the photographers couldn't keep up. Every few hundred feet he was forced to find three inches of ledge and pause there while the photographers repositioned their ropes and gear.

"How is Alex handling all of this newfound fame?" I asked. "Being on the cover of *National Geographic* is no joke."

The photographer thought for a few seconds and then said, "Well, I think Alex's point of view is, 'I am going to climb mountains, because that's what I do; I'm a mountain climber. So if you want to come along and take photos of me and pay me money to do it, that's cool. I was going to do this anyway.'"

Alex was going to climb mountains. That's what he does. That's who he is. His road to awesome is just like yours except it's vertical. And if you ever see a video of him, you'll know instantly that he's doing the right thing. On the ground he's kind of awkward. He seems uncomfortable and completely out of his element. On the mountain he transforms.

He was going to do it anyway.

How about you? What were you going to do anyway?

We all have something like that. We all have a passion or two like Alex. For me, it's creating ideas. I love that I get paid to write books and consult with companies. Both are a lot of fun. But regardless of the money, I was going to do those things anyway.

Because I'm a writer. That's what writers do. They share ideas.

## WHO DO YOU NEED TO BE WHEN YOU ENTER THE LAND OF MASTERING?

My friend Thad Cockrell gave me the answer. He's a musician.

A few months ago he started a new project called *Leagues*. After a successful solo career, he decided to strike out on a new adventure with a brand-new band.

Before they started recording the album, he called the guitar player and the drummer and the keyboard player and the audio engineer and anyone who was even remotely going to be involved with the project, and he told them who he needed them to be.

Their secret selves.

Call by call, he'd say, "I need you to be your secret self on this album. I need you to be the person you've always known you could be deep down inside but were afraid to be. The person you've always dreamed of being. I need that person on this album. I need you to be your secret self."

That's what I need you to be as we enter the land of Mastering.

It's time to be your secret self.

# MASTERING

## YOU READY FOR A BAR FIGHT?

I don't think I'm supposed to use the phrase "bar fight" as a Christian, but in this case, my hands are really tied. Can you think of another phrase that means "stool getting broken over someone's back"? I can't. Maybe "potluck fight" or "church picnic brawl," but neither of those captures the fury of an old-fashioned bar fight. And awesome is always up for one of those.

A dream you don't have to fight for isn't a dream—it's a nap. And while naps are delightful and enjoyed best on Sunday afternoon, they do very little to move you closer to awesome. A nap changes your afternoon. Awesome changes your world. Which is why I had a bar fight with Dave Ramsey.

When I wanted to name my last book *Quitter*, he pushed back. He felt that it was a bit too negative and wouldn't make a great title. We went round and round via a few emails until finally we decided to have a meeting.

I was a nervous wreck. I think at some point I won't be intimidated by Dave Ramsey anymore—probably around 2032 that will happen. But he's sold millions of books, has a personality that fills arenas, and spends every week giving five million people advice via his radio show. He's an entrepreneur who, after clawing his way back from bankruptcy, has spent the last twenty years building a successful business, fighting and scrapping the entire time.

The weekend before the meeting, I practiced the mini speech I was going to give him. On Saturday afternoon, I set up an office in my home so I could rehearse how I would sit and what I would do with my arms. Do I lean on my left while pointing with my right for emphasis, which is my power arm? Do I cross my arms to establish my seriousness, or is that bad body language?

I had everything ready for our meeting at 4:30 p.m. that Monday. At 9:35 a.m., my phone rang. It was my team leader, who said, "Hey, Dave is in my office and wants to talk about the title of your book." Ohhhh, time change. Well played, Dave Ramsey. Well played indeed.

So I marched up to the office, sweaty and a little throw-uppy. I sat down and told him why the title had to be *Quitter*. I told him I'd quit six of the eight jobs I've had in my life. I told him that, of the other two, I was fired from one and asked to leave the other. I laid out the grossness of my previous employment history as proof that I was indeed a quitter. I was anxious about what he'd say when he heard my background, but I had to fight for the title I believed in. It mattered to me, and I didn't know how much until I got into a fight about it.

His pushback helped me define my dream. It called out new passion and new energy for the title and the book. I'd presented a dozen other weak titles to the team, but I didn't care about them. It wasn't until I was pushed into the corner and forced to fight that my dream about the book really started to crystallize.

That's how the road to awesome works.

You're gonna get your hands dirty in a bar fight. You're gonna step into the fray of a meeting and throw some elbows. Awesome is not a casual affair. There's always some degree of scuffle. Some degree of opposition. And as long as you're pursuing your true awesome, you won't shrink from a fight.

Welcome to the land of Mastering. It's time to throw some elbows.

## I SPENT SOME TIME IN REHAB

In 2008, I decided I wanted to be a public speaker. After writing, it was the second thing I wanted to learn how to master.

I had hope, passion, and great gobs of desire to be a public speaker.

The only problem was that no one else cared.

Nobody would book me to come speak. And that was a good decision on their part. I was horrible.

But I was caught in a vicious cycle not unlike the one college graduates discover when they hit the real world looking for a job. This cycle is not uncommon when you enter the land of Mastering: You don't have any experience. The only way to get experience is to get a job. But every job for which you apply insists you still need experience. And around again you go.

Then I found a loophole in the system. It was in the last place most people would look—rehab.

A church near us had a residential rehab program. They had twelve people living in the facility at any given time. They were always looking for speakers because no one aims at the rehab crowd.

When you aspire to be a public speaker, you aim for huge crowds with huge stages and huge paychecks. Speaking to twelve people, who are in the throes of one of the worst seasons of their lives, for free, is not exactly a moment you aspire to. So why did I do it?

## It was awesome.

One of my dreams is to share hope with people. Talk about a group who needed some encouragement. Sometimes we get so caught up in waiting for the perfect context—the one we've always had in our heads—in order to begin being awesome. It's a horrible mistake. Awesome starts the moment you do what you love. If you truly love doing it, the environment in which you do it shouldn't matter (remember the Apple customer service rep?).

## They won't let you phone it in.

People in rehab are learning how to communicate honestly. They won't let you come in and sleepwalk through a speech. I had to dig deep and speak from my heart. That was an invaluable experience.

## Nobody else was doing it.

Do you know how many other public speakers asked the rehab center if they could speak there the same month I did? Zero. For someone who was horrible at public speaking, that was the level of competition I was ready to handle.

I only got to do it a couple times, but I loved it. And a few years after I spoke there, someone approached me after an event. He said, "I heard you the first time you spoke. I was in rehab, and that meant a lot to me."

Want to be more awesome at whatever it is you've chosen to master? Find your version of rehab—somewhere you can practice being awesome.

## GET EXPERIENCE

If you're not trying to be a public speaker, what does "rehab" look like for you? The three best things you can do to get some experience are:

### Volunteer.
### Take a part-time job.
### Be led.

None of those options are particularly sexy, but they are incredibly effective.

### Volunteer.

Sometimes my friends will tell me, "I'm starting a nonprofit!" I'll ask them what that means, and they'll say, "I registered a Twitter account and bought a URL, and I might do a kickstarter campaign."

"Have you been to the country your nonprofit will focus on?"

"Yes, I spent four days there once."

"Have you ever worked with an organization that is already on the ground there?"

"No. Why?"

And that's when I beg them to volunteer first.

I hope you start a million nonprofits. I hope you start a million businesses. I hope you start many different things. But don't be so eager to rush through the land of Mastering that you refuse to volunteer.

We think a six-month period of volunteering will delay us from our dream.

We are wrong.

Volunteering does not slow you down. It speeds you up. It gives you a crash-course education that will be invaluable once you launch whatever it is you want to launch. It teaches you lessons you'd rather learn when your future isn't at stake.

Am I recommending you quit your day job today and volunteer for six months? No. I'm suggesting that, in the land of Mastering, you make a conscious, deliberate effort to find a volunteer sign-up sheet. It doesn't have to be a soup kitchen. Throw out your old definition of "volunteer." The new definition of volunteer is "any activity that lets you trade time for expertise."

That can be almost anything. My friend Jeff Goins wanted to be an awesome blogger. So instead of just focusing on his blog, he created a very intentional list of blogs he would guest post for. For more than a year, he wrote guest posts for free for other blogs.

Did he get better at blogging?

You bet.

Did his volunteering lead to great relationships in the blogging community?

Absolutely.

Did his own blog, his awesome, grow as a result of his volunteering?

Significantly.

Would yours too?

There's no doubt.

## Take a part-time job.

One morning, while waiting for a taxi in a hotel lobby, I talked with a driver who had come to pick up someone else. He was a nice guy and proceeded to tell me a few stories about his life in Florida. Out of work, he had taken the driving job as a stopgap. His house was upside down, his prospects were nonexistent, and he described Florida much like Vin Diesel's character in *The Chronicles of Riddick* would have described the prison planet he escaped from.

After a few minutes, my ride came and I jumped in the back of the car. I figured he'd have a story much like the first driver. After all, they were in the exact same profession, in the exact same geography, in the exact same economy. Instead, when I asked him how he was doing, this is what he said:

"Things are great! So much opportunity down here. We moved from up north, and we absolutely love Florida! I started this driving business, and it's really starting to grow."

I was confused by these two completely different experiences, so I told him, "I just talked to another driver, and he told me the exact opposite story. What's different about you? Same city, same profession, same economy. Where's the disconnect?"

He laughed a little and then told me his story.

One day he hired a driver to pick up his family at the airport. He wanted his kids to have the fun experience of having someone waiting for you at baggage claim with your name on a sign. He was looking forward to the whole experience, but it turned out to be pretty lackluster. The driver wasn't kind, the service was average, and the cost was high.

After thinking about it for a while, he reached a conclusion that a lot of new business owners reach: "I bet I could do that better."

He could provide better service at a better price and probably build a much better business.

And here's where his story gets awesome.

He could have very easily said to his wife, "I've never been a driver. I've never worked for a driving service. I know nothing about that business. I'm going to do some light research, online mostly, and then throw our life savings, all our stability, our kids' futures, and anything not bolted down in our home at this new dream of mine. Then, six months later, when things don't grow as fast as I planned, I'm going to act shocked that you're uncomfortable with this dream."

Instead, he ignored the average path and got a job at the same car company from which his family got that lackluster ride. Instead of just getting theory training, he got on-the-job training. He spent four months learning the ins and outs of that business. He worked as hard as he could for his new employer, and in turn, he got to learn what it means to run a driving service company.

Then, and only then, did he decide to start his company.

If you've got a dream that involves a business of any kind, don't be too proud, impatient, or foolish to think you don't need a part-time job. Why learn your mistakes when the stakes are the absolute highest? Why attach your entire future to an experiment? Why not get a paid-for education in your dream?

If you want to start a coffeehouse but have never worked at one in your entire life, you need to work at Starbucks first. Maybe you will come to hate coffee. Maybe you'll get sick of retail hours. Maybe opening a store at 4:30 a.m. every morning will be a nightmare by month two.

I'd rather you find that out in your part-time job than your full-time dream.

## Be led.

Sometimes people get in my ear. Not literally, but metaphorically. And under the guise of advice, they'll say some interesting things. Here is something I've heard a few times: "Wow, I'm surprised you joined Dave Ramsey's team. You could be doing all of this blog and book stuff on your own by now. Why didn't you just start your own thing?"

Sometimes when people say that they mean it as a compliment of sorts. They mean I've written a book and have a blog and a Twitter account, and maybe it's really time to strike out on my own. Sometimes they mean it as a dig, that I have somehow taken the easy route or safe route or cowardly route by joining someone else's team instead of going solo.

I've been thinking about those comments for a year now, and I think they represent an interesting shift in our culture. On one end of the spectrum is the entrepreneur, who feels called to go it alone. There are so many tools and opportunities right now for sailing your own ship. This is an amazing time to be an entrepreneur and, for many people, that is the perfect decision.

Sometimes, however, along the way a sense of impatience and even entitlement gets tangled with our sense of entrepreneurship. We're so desperate to be "the man" or "the woman" right away. We're so eager to chart our own course that we don't think we need to be led. We say, "I can grow my own platform easily with social media . . . I can get my own following . . . I've been called to do this, and nobody in the history of mankind has ever done it like this! Who could possibly give me advice? Being an apprentice would be failure. This is my time!"

With that line of thinking, we've climbed an entitlement ladder and lost a few things.

We've lost the value of wise counsel.

We've lost the honor of sitting under someone else's leadership.

We've lost the joy of building something slowly that impacts multiple generations instead of just our own lives.

Why did I decide to work for Dave Ramsey?

Because I want to be led. I want to learn from a master. I want to admit time and time again, "I don't know the best way to do this. Will you teach me?"

I have a new thought now when people tell me, "Wow, I'm surprised you joined Dave Ramsey's team." Now in my head, I think, *You're right. He spent two decades growing a business from zero employees to more than 300 and building a radio empire that's on 500 radio stations across the country. I've written a blog and a couple books. We're pretty much on the same level at this point. I'm done learning and should probably step out on my own already. What could that guy possibly teach me?*

Be led. Be taught. Remain a learner.

Don't ever avoid opportunities to gain more experience and wisdom just because you're "mastering" something. Learning from those before you is a dying art that can catapult you ahead in the land of Mastering.

## NOW, DO THE REPS

I am racing the sun, but I will not win.

I am desperate for it to go down, but since it's 3:00 p.m. and I'm about to take the stage, it's probably not going to happen. I suppose if the sunset were at three in the afternoon, we'd have bigger issues than me bombing at a music festival, but I'm pretty selfish, so I wasn't thinking about the ramifications of a solar apocalypse at that moment.

I was thinking about the smattering of high schoolers who were expecting to see a rapper named Lecrae and instead got me. You've never seen such disappointed teenagers in your life.

It was the first and only music festival I've ever spoken at. I knew the second we booked it that it was going to be tough, but I didn't know how tough.

Part of the challenge was that it was in the middle of the day. At least if it had been night, there would've been a spotlight visually guiding people to the stage. The other part of the challenge was a punk band playing on another stage at the same time. People liked punk in droves when they realized the headlining rapper was not coming out until after some guy speaking.

The music festival was fantastic for music, but I'm not a band. And when you speak, you can always find the person in the crowd who is most disappointed with whatever it is you're saying. Out of a crowd of a thousand, you'll have hater-seeking vision for the person asleep, frowning, or shaking his head back and forth as a means of shot-blocking your words back to the stage.

I saw him pretty quickly too. He was about 18 years old and leaning against the security barrier at the front of the stage. I tried to look away, but I kept seeing him in the crowd over and over again, staring and willing me off the stage with a scowl that would have rivaled my own at that age. Mid-speech, I realized the problem; he was a twin. I wasn't just seeing him. I was seeing him and his identical twin brother. I can only assume that they were like Xamot and Tomax from *GI Joe* because it was clear they were able to feel each other's pain.

It was a brutal event until I realized something really simple during the middle of my speech. I was doing a rep.

That's how you reach awesome.

You do reps.

How do you become a master?

You do reps.

If you want to get better at something, you have to do the reps. That's true for almost every part of life.

Want to be great friends with someone? Do the reps. Go to coffee. Help them move. Stop by on random Tuesday nights. Stack up enough reps until you have the relationship you want. We tend to think it works the other way around. That if we want to have a great friendship, we need to do great moments together. And those are important, but those are few and far between. Every coffee you have with a close friend will not be a moment you journal about later. "Dear diary, Jill cried at coffee today again. We shared our hearts over huckleberry scones and solved several of our problems through the power of conversation and transparency."

More often than not, you'll just have coffee. You'll just talk and laugh. You'll just do a rep.

And one day you'll look up and realize you have an awesome friendship.

Dreams work the same way. You don't get to pick and choose a life of home-run moments. You get to swing the bat, a lot. Some of them are going to connect; some of them won't. But each one takes you one step closer to awesome.

That's why I do reps.

That's why I wrote millions of words on my blog.

That's why some weeks of the year, I'll speak six different times on six different days to six different audiences with six different messages.

That's why I had twenty-six 1099s in 2010.

I had a full-time job and I liked it. But I wanted to get better at freelance writing. I needed to do some reps.

We often think talent is the key to awesome. But if you pull the curtain back on most of the people we'd call "geniuses," what you find is an incredible amount of hard work. Take Mozart: "By the time he was 28 years old, his hands were deformed because of all the hours he had spent practicing, performing, and gripping a quill pen to compose."

Yay! Claw hands! That sounds great, Jon. Good sell on the value of hard work.

The point isn't to acquire claw hands—it's to add hustle to your talent. As author Twyla Tharp says, "Mozart was hardly some naïve prodigy who sat down at the keyboard and, with God whispering in his ears, let the music flow from his fingertips. It's a nice image for selling tickets to movies, but whether or not God has kissed your brow, you still have to work. Without learning and preparation, you won't know how to harness the power of that kiss."[1]

If you're going to make your way through the land of Mastering, go to rehab, volunteer, take a part-time job, and above all, do the reps.

## SOME THINGS ARE HOBBIES, AND THAT'S OKAY

If everything goes according to plan, I will never participate in a triathlon. I will never find myself stripping off a wetsuit upon emerging from a lake or ocean and jumping on a bike with a complicated name and a poorly padded seat. I will never end a grueling day of bike riding with a half marathon or full marathon. I've had that goal of not being in a triathlon for years and so far have been able to accomplish it.

I'm happy that a lot of my friends love triathlons. For some people, that type of exercise is part of their awesome, but it's not part of mine. Though I like running, it's not something I'm trying to master. It's not something I want to put through the five stages of awesome. It's a hobby, and that's okay.

You'll have some hobbies too—things that you have fun doing but don't really want to master. Hopefully in the land of Mastering a few come to mind. "Do I really care enough about _____ to do the reps or volunteer or get a part-time job?" Maybe you don't. Maybe what looked like part of your awesome at the beginning of the map has actually revealed itself to be a hobby.

That's not failure. That's success, because now you know where to put that particular activity. Give up any guilt you have about your inability to start a quilting business. Maybe quilting is just for you. It's a small hobby that brings you big happiness. And recognizing that, you can now focus on the things in your life that you want to take beyond a hobby. The things you want to master and harvest and guide.

The things that define your awesome.

## IGNORE THE BULLHORNS, FOR NOW

The road through Mastering is littered with bullhorns. Don't pick them up. They're only going to distract you from one of the other keys to mastering your passion. If you grab the bullhorn too soon, you won't learn that to be awesome you need to spend more time practicing your dream than you do promoting your dream.

The Internet has made it ridiculously easy to promote your dream, your craft, your passion, your whatever. But that ease comes with a consequence.

The temptation is to spend more time on promoting what you're doing instead of practicing what you're doing. Mastering your skills, putting in the hours to become great, working hard while no one is watching. Promoting makes people think you're already a master. Practicing is what actually makes you a master. There's a huge difference between the two.

Want to stand out from the clutter of social media and be awesome? Spend ten hours practicing your dream for every one hour you spend promoting it.

Want to be awesome even faster? Make that ratio 100 to 1.

## THERE WILL BE HATERS

Someone is going to hate what you do. That's not a maybe. That's a definite. And I don't mean dislike. I mean hate. With energy and vitriol and a passion that surprises you.

Haters are inevitable. Your response is up for grabs.

The first thing we need to do as we navigate this section of the map is draw a clear distinction between hate and constructive criticism.

Hate leads to a wound.

*Constructive criticism leads to an improvement.*

Hate's motive is to hurt.

*Constructive criticism's motive is to help.*

Hate is an anchor.

*Constructive criticism is a gift.*

If you confuse the two, you'll spend far too much time trying to find a vitamin in the poison of hate, and you'll miss the benefit of constructive criticism because you interpret it as an attack.

To further distinguish the two, I want you to ask two quick questions the next time your dream gets hated on. You have to ask them immediately before the hate has time to settle in your head and confuse you into thinking it's constructive criticism.

## Question #1: Who said it?

Was it a close friend or a complete stranger? A business colleague or someone driving by you on the highway? It sounds ridiculous that you'd need to ask this question, but you do. Most of us receive all hate as if we're receiving it from someone who knows us deeply. In the heat of the moment, we act as if this person can see deep into our soul and their words carry truth.

Case in point, a few months ago I got some hate mail. Instead of stopping to ask, "Who said it?" I immediately wrote a long response. I wrestled with it emotionally for hours, never once answering this first question. If I had, I would have quickly realized a stranger said it. Someone who has never met me, had a conversation with me, Skyped with me, or had any interaction with me. So why was I giving his words such power?

When someone leaves a hateful comment on your blog or tweets about you, that's the equivalent of someone driving by your house and yelling, "I hate your yard! Your heart must be horrible too!" You'd never listen to that person in real life. Don't listen online.

## Question #2: Why did they say it?

What was their motive? Were they exposing a blind spot in my life so that I might improve something I was doing? Or are they mad about something completely different and just looking to lash out at anyone who gets in their path?

Pausing to ask why gives you time to reflect before you act. I once worked with a guy who was really angry and combative. It would have been easy to label the way he acted as hate. But when I stopped to ask, "Why does he say the things he says?" I learned his wife had breast cancer. That wasn't hate bubbling up; that was hurt. That was fear and hopelessness. His hate didn't have anything to do with me and, instead, had everything to do with a terrible situation he was facing. Once I knew that, he became invisible as a hater and visible as a guy who needed a friend.

Asking those two questions is all it takes to make 99 percent of all haters invisible.

Who?

Why?

Six simple letters.

Next time you get hate, make sure it's not valuable criticism from someone who is trying to help you get better. Once you've identified who said it and why they said it, chances are you can stop worrying about it and brush the dirt off your shoulder.

## CRITIC'S MATH

We've already removed 99 percent of all hate. There's only 1 percent left. We're so efficient! Only there's a problem: 1 percent is all it takes to steer you off the path to awesome and right back to average.

It's a math issue, really, but it starts with how we handle compliments. Most people can't stand to get a compliment. The first thing we do is try to deny it. We reject it quickly and say things like:

"Oh, that was nothing."

"It's a lot easier than it looks."

"It wasn't that hard."

We discount compliments and make sure they don't have a second to touch down on the road of awesome we're traveling. We ignore them and keep walking.

But when someone insults us or hates on what we're doing, we have a very different reaction. Suddenly, we stop everything else we're working on and focus on the hate.

We give it our best attention. We give it our best focus. We give it our best energy.

This person *gets* us. They really know what they are talking about. We need to laser right in on this and spend some time on what they said. In those moments, we tend to believe in critic's math. And it's a simple formula, because I'm not good at math. Here's what it is:

1 insult + 1,000 compliments = 1 insult

Did you catch it?

In the face of 1,000 compliments and only one insult, you and I will only have eyes for the negative.

That sounds silly, but I promise you it is true. I've seen it hundreds of times across the country. When I consult with businesses, you would be amazed at how much time and money they spend trying to fix one unhappy customer's experience. They will hold SWAT team meetings to address Steve-in-Detroit's problem while at the same time ignoring the 1,000 fans who love what their business does.

And I am not immune to this either. At the time I wrote this book, my third book, *Quitter*, had 160 five-star reviews on Amazon and three one-star reviews. Can you guess which ones I have memorized?

Critic's math is something everyone struggles with, even people who are proven experts in their field. Larry David is the cocreator of *Seinfeld*, one of the most successful sitcoms in the history of television. He also has a hit show on HBO called *Curb Your Enthusiasm*. One night while waiting for a flight, I grabbed a copy of *Rolling Stone* because he was on the cover. To say that he is successful by any measurement would be an understatement.

As I sat there on the plane, I got a peek at how Larry David, one of the most accomplished men in television today, handles critic's math.

One day, David had a homecoming in New York. He lives in LA now to film his show. While he was in town he went to a Yankees game. During the middle of the game the stadium managers found out he was in the crowd. As a tribute, they showed his picture on the big screen and played the theme song to his show over the loudspeakers. What a moment! The author of the article captures it perfectly: "An entire stadium of fans stood and cheered for the hopeless case from Brooklyn. It should have been a life-defining moment, the redemptive final scene in the biopic."

Alas, in the midst of that tremendous win, critic's math reared its ugly head. At the end of the night, while Larry was walking to his car, a stranger drove by and yelled, "Larry, you suck!"

Can you guess who Larry thought about on the ride home? Can you guess who he talked about? Can you guess who dominated that day for him?

The stranger who told him he sucked.[2]

Critic's math made an entire stadium disappear. Critic's math made 50,000 people invisible. David Blaine can't pull that off. David Copperfield can't do that trick. Criss Angel is not capable of that.

That's how powerful critic's math is.

Larry spent the ride back from the Bronx obsessing over that moment, running it over and over in his mind. It was as if the other 50,000 people, the ones who loved him, didn't exist. "Who's that guy? What was that?" he asked. "Who would do that? Why would you say something like that?"

The tricky thing about critic's math is:

### It doesn't instantly go away with success.

If right now you're thinking, *If I sell a certain number of books or get a job promotion, I won't worry so much about what critics think*, you're wrong. If you had a hard time with critic's math with ten followers on Twitter, you'll still have a hard time with 1 million followers. Don't chase success as a way to beat critic's math. You'll only hurt yourself.

### Every time you believe critic's math, you make it more powerful.

Fear and doubt are like muscles. Every time you believe a lie, it gets easier to believe the next time.

Knowing that it's poison, how do we beat it?

Let's look to the founder of Southwest Airlines, Herb Kelleher, for a brilliant suggestion.

Years ago, there was a woman who wrote so many letters of complaint to Southwest that she became nicknamed "Pen Pal" around the corporate headquarters. After every flight, she mailed in a complaint. She hated that there was no first class. She wanted a meal. She wanted to have assigned seats. Letter after letter hit Southwest. The company prided themselves on answering every correspondence from customers, but nothing they said would satisfy this customer.

Her last letter, reciting a litany of complaints, momentarily stumped Southwest's customer relations people. They bumped it up to Herb's desk with a note: "This one's yours."

Now, the majority of CEOs are going to read that letter and send that offended customer a stack of free drink coupons. Ease the customer's pain with a gift. Instead, Herb Kelleher took sixty seconds out of his day and wrote the woman back a four-word message. They are four words I want you to keep in mind when critic's math gets loud. He wrote, "We will miss you."[3]

Your dream will not be for everyone. Your road to awesome is not all-inclusive. There are going to be some haters who lob rocks at you from deep in the land of Mastering. The temptation will be to stop along your journey and engage with them. To turn their rocks into an altar and offer up something that will ease their frustration with you. You will be tempted to try to win them back to your side. To explain your case to them. Ignore this temptation. In the face of critic's math, be like Herb. Say, "We will miss you," and then keep moving so your words are true as you leave the haters behind you.

## THE LAST STOP IN THE LAND OF MASTERING

In the summer of 2010, I got empty.

Sensing the imminent arrival of burnout, I spent ten days turning everything off. I didn't do anything on social media. But do you know what that felt like? Every day of 2003. And also every day of the first thirty years of my life. (The pats on the back we give ourselves for not using social media for brief moments of time are ridiculous.)

The biggest thing I did was turn off my ideas. For years, I believed I was an idea guy, and coming up with new ideas was how I relaxed on vacation. Ideas were a big part of my awesome, and it only seemed right that I would take them on vacation with me. I'd use time off to brainstorm, focus on new plans for the future, read a ton of self-help or business books, and get ahead on any projects I was working on. Then I'd return from vacation completely exhausted and wonder why.

But this time I spent those ten days reading nothing but fiction. I put down my journals and my iPhone. I built sandcastles on the beach with my kids. I had long conversations with my wife. I tried not to write horrible poetry about ocean waves.

It was awesome, and for the first time in years I came home empty, but full of life.

A week later I told my friend Al Andrews about the experience. He smiled and said, "Wow! That's great! Now, how do you do that next Tuesday? How do you do that next month without a beach? How do you make sure you don't kill yourself for fifty weeks of the year with the hope that you can make it to those two weeks of vacation?"

I told him I didn't know.

Without missing a beat, he said, "You need to build your own Central Park."

I had no idea what that meant, so he explained the idea.

"Well," he said, "if you fly over New York City, Central Park kind of looks like this wasted green space. There in the heart of this bustling city is this lump of grass. Imagine all the buildings and commerce and innovation we could put on that space! But New York City knows that, without Central Park, it would combust. It would implode and collapse on itself without that space, that sanctuary. The problem is that most people have put buildings on top of every part of their lives. They have no Central Park in their day or their week or their month. That's how you've been living, Jon. It's time to knock down some buildings. You need to cultivate your own Central Park."

That conversation and challenge changed my life. I started building my own Central Park. I started going to a botanical garden in town. I started taking regular fiction breaks. I started running more. I started to knock down some buildings.

You are going to work harder than you ever have on the road to awesome. You are going to do reps and volunteer and edit and learn and a million other things. But make sure that in the midst of this adventure you don't confuse "building up your dream" with "burning out your dream." Don't be afraid to take a break. To walk away from what you're doing to catch your breath. To knock down a few buildings. That's one more tension you'll have to embrace on the road to awesome—the need to both hustle and rest. It's an important one because there's too much fun to be had in the land of Harvesting for us to burn out before we even get there.

And when we do get there, let's make sure we're careful about one more thing—our expectations. If we're not honest about them, we'll wreck the land of Harvesting, like I wrecked my honeymoon.

Weeks before we flew to Jamaica as newlyweds, Jenny told me a story that shaped the entire week for me. A girl she worked with went to a similar Sandals resort. While at the all-inclusive vacation destination, she and her husband met another couple enjoying their honeymoon. Over a period of sun-soaked Caribbean days, the two couples became great friends. They dined together, snorkeled together, and played shuffleboard together. When the trip was over, they returned to the States not just with new marriages, but with new best friends.

Years later they still got together to celebrate their friendship.

My fiancee said that to me in passing, but in the moment I started to grow an expectation in my head: "Jenny and I will make lifelong best friends on our honeymoon."

That only sounds stupid because it was, but in my defense, it's difficult to make "couple friends." It's hard to find another couple you click with on everything. Just when you think you've found someone both husband and wife love hanging out with, they tell you they own a ferret farm they call "Ferretopia." Recognizing that challenge even before I got married, I decided to look for a shortcut. And lo and behold, one was presented to me in the form of my honeymoon.

Who knew that a honeymoon could be such a treasure trove of friendships?

In the weeks leading up to the honeymoon, my expectation that we would meet our best friends in Jamaica began to grow.

I didn't tell anyone; I just quietly watered it with hope and foolishness. By the time we landed in Jamaica, my expectation was no longer small and adorable—it was a monster of massive proportions. As we sat down on the bus to the resort, I started eyeballing the other passengers.

*Who here looks like they could be our lifelong couple friends? Those two over there look pretty interesting . . . he's got cool sunglasses on . . . she seems pretty normal. Based on how she's sitting on a bus. It's an admittedly small sample group of information, but it's all I have to work with right now.*

I continued to plot and plan this way during the entire drive. That night, when we got to the hotel, I asked my wife if there was anyone she wanted to invite to dinner.

She seemed a little taken back by this question, like maybe she hadn't been doing best-friend recon. She seemed to think, *Yes. You. My husband of twenty-four hours. That's who I would like to go to dinner with.*

Good to know. Apparently I was the only one committed to this friendship mission. The rest of the week I kept trying to initiate lifelong friendship conversations with anyone who made eye contact with me. It wasn't easy. A lot of the people there seemed to be distracted by their new spouses or something.

Finally recognizing that we'd already missed our shot at the two coolest couples there that week—they paired off on day two, much to my poolside chagrin—I asked a different couple to dinner with us.

We had absolutely nothing in common with them. They were both from small towns and had never been to the big city before. When their car got broken into in downtown Birmingham, Alabama, the wife assumed a bomb had been planted in it. People in cities are constantly planting bombs in used Accords on the fifth floor of parking garages. She wouldn't get in the car until the husband had inspected it. What sort of bomb-inspecting skills he possessed was never fully discussed, but I assume they boiled down to just looking for big red sticks of dynamite with a slowly burning fuse.

I knew in the first five minutes that we were in for a long night and probably weren't going to call each other after we got back from our honeymoons, but it didn't matter.

I was desperate. My expectation was a monster that had mutated into a demand. And demands will suck the beauty out of anything if you let them grow, even honeymoons.

On the flight home, sensing my dejected spirit, my brand-new wife asked me what was wrong. I confessed my great disappointment that we had never managed to make new best friends during our honeymoon. She quietly looked down at her left hand and tried to see if she could slide the ring off without causing a scene.

She couldn't. The diamond I bought her was so large and heavy she could barely lift her arm, never mind her finger. We landed. I got over it. But something was lost.

The joy of that week was tarnished. As silly as that whole story is, my expectation came with a cost. I missed some of that week because I was lost inside my expectation. I had so overbuilt my expectation that it was impossible for life to deliver. I had created this stock photography version of my honeymoon, and the second it didn't meet that, I started to feel like I had failed my honeymoon.

The same thing will happen to you in the land of Harvesting if you're not careful.

When we realize that expectations can cause damage, our natural response is to think, *Stupid expectations. I'll fix this by never having any!* But that doesn't work. It's impossible to have zero expectations. Try as you might, you are going to carry at least a thread of expectation into every part of your life.

The other reason it doesn't work is that all too often it becomes a protectionist move. You think, *I'll go in with low expectations. If they're met or exceeded, then great! I'll be pleasantly surprised. If they're not? I won't be disappointed.* And on the surface that sounds okay, but over time, that approach tends to morph into you thinking, *If I get my hope up and it doesn't come true, I'll be hurt. So I'll protect myself from being hurt by not having any hope or expectations. I'll hurt myself first before the situation has a chance to.*

Maybe you're wired differently than I am. Maybe you can compare your expectations to the experience and not feel like at least a little bit of a failure, but I have my doubts.

I think you need crazy expectations. You can't dream without creating expectations, and they can be an encouraging source of motivation. Expectations of the future can inspire you to reach for things that feel impossible in the present. As you get ready to open your business, write your book, finish your college degree, or any number of things, I want you to take huge, wild expectations into that. I want you to throw expectation after expectation into the furnace of your life until there is a bonfire of excitement that rivals the sun in intensity.

But after expectation has played its role, after you've squeezed every last drop of encouragement out of it, I want you to then let it go as you leave the land of Mastering and enter the land of Harvesting.

There are going to be some crops you harvest that wildly exceed your expectations. There will be surprises—both good and bad—that you could not have possibly foreseen when you started down the road to awesome. We agreed at the beginning of this book that you can't control the finish line; you can only control the starting line. Well, now we're toward the end of our journey. What you've sown and grown will now come to fruition. Don't ruin it with unmet expectations you refuse to let go of in the face of the fun things that actually do happen. And don't act like it doesn't matter and use apathy as a protective shield. The things you harvest do matter—that's the joy of doing work that matters. Enjoy the harvest.

# HARVESTING

**JUST INSIDE THE BORDER** of the land of Harvesting, there is an exit. The path is wide, the road is easy, and you will have barely taken a step into Harvesting before you see it plain as day. And if you take it now, if you explore it at this point, you will undo all the awesome you've set into motion thus far.

What is the exit? Turns out it's a simple secret, and it holds the answer to more than you think.

## HOW TO BE AN AWESOME PUBLIC SPEAKER AND JUST ABOUT EVERYTHING ELSE TOO

Want to know the secret to being an awesome public speaker? Want to know how to book more gigs, make more money, and do more repeat business? Want to know how to play in the NFL past your prime? Want to know how to be awesome at just about everything else too? It's simple.

Don't be a jerk.

If you want to take a moment and scribble that on a note you hang on the fridge, I'll wait before unpacking it.

That gem may not be new knowledge to you, but it was to me. I learned it backstage at dozens of speaking events.

I thought the only fuel that drove awesome was talent. I thought if you really wanted to be awesome at something, you just had to stockpile enough talent or skill in any given industry or career. But then I started to have conversations with clients who booked me to speak.

I'd go speak at the event, step off stage, and end up in quick conversations on the way back to the airport. The host of the event wouldn't talk much about what I said from stage. They wouldn't comment on the content of my speech. They wouldn't point out an idea I shared. Instead, they all said the same thing: "Thanks for being so nice!"

Turns out, there's a large population of jerk speakers and jerk musicians traveling about the country, making my job incredibly easy. They berate the staff at events, refuse to do Q&A sessions with conference attendees, and hide in their hotels instead of taking photos or shaking hands or break dancing. Sometimes they even refuse to speak until the room is full. If that's you, let me simply say, thank you.

What a gift you have given me and every other public speaker on the planet who is not a jerk. You've created such a low bar of kindness that a toddler could jump over it with the greatest of ease.

When people compliment me for being nice, they are usually not remarking on some grand show of kindness I have performed from stage. I have not sent them bouquets of flowers. I have not purchased them a vehicle or carved a tree stump that was struck by lightning into the shape of their college's mascot.

I just haven't been a jerk.

I wish it were more difficult than that, but it's not.

If you want to harvest more awesome, don't take the jerkdome exit, which you'll see a thousand times in the land of Harvesting. Stay the course so that when you arrive in the land of Guiding, there will actually be someone to guide.

People don't like working with jerks. They don't listen to jerks. People don't do favors for jerks. Because people don't want jerks to win.

That's something Terrell Owens discovered the hard way. He's one of the greatest wide receivers in the history of the NFL. He's second in career receiving yards only to Jerry Rice. He's caught more than 1,000 touchdowns, something only eight other people can claim. He is a six-time Pro Bowler. And on the day I wrote this page, he was released from the Allen Wranglers—not an NFL franchise—an arena football team.

How did he end up there?

As a *GQ* profile reported, it's "hard to live down the reputation as a team poison." And NFL executives have long memories. "It's not his knee that's the problem; it's his attitude," said one executive from one of the better teams, who didn't want to be named. The ratio that once made it worth it for owners to sign him— two parts genius to two parts trouble—has shifted now that he's not quite as fast and his body is not as reliable. "With T. O., no matter how brilliant he can be on the field, the dark side is always lurking. You don't know which T. O. you're going to get, and no one is comfortable risking that."[1]

Whether you're in the NFL or a cubicle, the same truth about being a jerk holds: wild talent and a bad attitude eventually lose to mild talent and a good attitude.

And the sad thing is that the "eventually" tends to occur in the land of Harvesting. These should be the years when Terrell Owens is harvesting the rewards of a long, productive career—statistically one of the best careers for a wide receiver in NFL history. He should be enjoying the fruits of his labor and soon heading to the land of Guiding to help other young receivers be awesome too. Or he could be on television, talking about his years in the NFL and offering expert insight. There are dozens and dozens of sports shows he could be on right now, harvesting his career.

Instead, he's getting fired from the Allen Wranglers.

Don't be a jerk. Avoid those exits with everything you've got.

## YOUR FIFTEEN MINUTES COULD COST YOU A LIFETIME

If you manage to walk down the road to awesome without becoming a jerk, then you'll successfully avoid the largest exit back to average. But you're not out of the woods yet. There's one more massive exit hidden in every land—but most prominently in Harvesting. It's called "fame."

In 1968, Andy Warhol said, "In the future, everyone will be world-famous for fifteen minutes."[2] At the time, that must have seemed like a ludicrous thought, but the Internet has proven Warhol a prophet.

With the click of a button, you've got access to the entire world. And with a single tweet or viral video, you can have your fifteen—or more—minutes of fame. You may not think your pursuit of awesome will ever generate any kind of fame for you, but you'd be surprised. Even if you've got a niche passion, there are people around the world who share that exact same passion. And if you decide to master it and harvest it, you will gain some degree of fame, no matter how small. The challenge is that a little fame can do a lot of damage.

The problem is that the minute you have a single fan or follower, people start to build an expectation of who you are. You're the funny guy or fashion-forward mom or sports enthusiast, and with that comes an expectation of how each of those people should act. You're smart and may enjoy the attention, so you begin playing up to that expectation. Now there's a divide starting to happen, and it's subtle, but it's there. You're now two people—the person you really are and the person the public sees. You start to maintain a public image, which is exhausting. Instead of actually continuing down the road to awesome, you build a façade of what it looks like to walk down the road of awesome. And the progress you've made takes a detour back to average as you get stuck chasing fame, not more awesome.

I almost didn't put this section in the book because the reality is that we won't all be famous. That's mathematically impossible. But we all have the tools to have a little bit of fame, and that's enough to wreck many a dream.

One time I ate a cheeseburger at a small restaurant in Franklin, Tennessee. When I got home, I saw on Twitter that the restaurant had tweeted about me being there. I'm not going to lie; that felt good. But do you know what happened the next time I went out to eat? I expected another tweet.

I started thinking, *Who is noticing that I'm in here? Who is watching me right now? I can't wait to check Twitter once I'm done with lunch to see who witnessed my greatness!*

I was able to generate that amount of distraction and insanity from a single tweet by a hamburger joint. Who knows what will happen if whatever bit of awesome you're harvesting lands you in the newspaper? Or if you end up on TV or at the top of a blogging empire?

Don't get me wrong; fame can be a wonderful harvest, and you can use it for good. Ask Bono about that. But don't let it be the exit that leads you right back to average.

## BOOOOOO

Buzzkill! This is the land of Harvesting! The hard work has been done. It's time to sit back and enjoy the fruit of all our labors! It's time to coast.

Only it's not. Ask a farmer someday if the harvest season is easy. And don't confuse Harvesting with retirement. Don't confuse Harvesting with vacation. Don't confuse Harvesting with the end of the story. That'd be like running a marathon and then lying down fifty feet from the finish line for a nap.

I tried that last year, and it didn't go very well for me.

## HOW TO LOSE 99 PERCENT OF YOUR PROGRESS

The problem with the entitlement ladder in the land of Harvesting is that you don't usually know you're on one until you fall off it. You don't realize how high you are and how disconnected from reality you are until you crash back down to earth. Or in my case, lose 99 percent of your Facebook fans.

At some point during 2011, I started climbing an entitlement ladder. The problem was that I started to get lazy because of my job.

I have been given a very unique opportunity. In 2010, Dave Ramsey essentially said, "I dare you to be awesome." Then he hired me and said, "Go for it." That was an intimidating proposition in some ways. It was way easier to complain and moan on the sidelines about what I could do if I weren't too busy. "I'd write so many books and speak at so many places and chase my dream so much if I only had the time." I could make bold statements like this because I had a day job that owned forty hours of my week.

Then Dave hired me and threw away the governor belt. He brought me into a 300-person company and said, "Let's see what you've got."

At which point I got lazy.

It snuck up on me; I swear it did. I didn't even see that ladder. But before I knew it, I was a few rungs up, coasting the day away, shouting down to all who could hear: "Look at me! I'm Jon Acuff! I work for Dave Ramsey!"

I started to believe that other people in the building would take care of things for me. My attitude became, "I'm an *author*, and I can only sully my hands with adjectives and perhaps the en dash or em dash." I started ignoring some important responsibilities. I quietly acted like *I* had a team of 300 people. Like maybe *I* had built the company.

But I hadn't. I'm a team member. I'm a small, small cog in a very big machine that is named Dave Ramsey, not Jon Acuff. And though I'd taken a few steps into Harvesting and was seeing opportunities crop up that I had set in motion four years earlier,

I started to coast. And in the process, I lost 99 percent of my Facebook fans.

When my book *Stuff Christians Like* came out, I started a Stuff Christians Like group on Facebook. I built the group to around 10,000 people. I hustled on it, participated in it, and worked hard to keep it going.

Then I got on the entitlement ladder and forgot it existed.

Surely someone else at Dave Ramsey's headquarters can monitor that. I'm Jon Acuff! People want my photo! I autograph Kindles. Not just books, Kindles!

A year later, after talking with a friend who reminded me that Facebook is roughly the size of the planet and only dumb people aren't actively using it to grow their projects, I checked out the Stuff Christians Like group.

The top of the page said: "Your group has been migrated."

*Hooray!* I thought. *I don't know what that means, but it sounds great!* Butterflies migrate to Mexico because it's nice and warm. Canada Geese, the most pretentious birds in the world, migrate to Tennessee because arctic foxes eat them on the tundra. Migration is always a good thing.

The Facebook message continued: "Now that your group has been upgraded to the new groups format, information from your old group is still available, including group posts and discussions." Fantastic so far!

"Admins from the old group will continue as members." Man, Zuckerberg, you've thought of everything! Thanks for that convenience.

"Only members who asked to stay in the group will continue as members."

Wait—what? What was that last part? What's that you say? Hmmm, that's a weird one that doesn't really sound like a benefit. But how bad could it be?

So I checked the number of members who stayed with me. And the answer was, "wicked bad."

The group originally had 10,000 members.

It now had 23.

I'm not great at math, but I'm almost positive that equates to a 99 percent loss. There were 10,000, and now there are 23. Karen, Leo, Nicole—I could name them all and not really take up a lot of space in this book.

The group was gone. While I climbed an entitlement ladder, one field that had taken me years to harvest died. I am certain Facebook gave me notifications. I am sure they warned me and gave me ample opportunity to keep the group going at the same size. But I was too high in the sky to be bothered with it.

And so I lost 9,977 people from my 10,000-person group.

This may not mean much to you. Maybe you've got a million people in your Facebook group. Or maybe you've never heard of Facebook and bought this book on what we call "paper." Doesn't matter a whole lot. This isn't about social media. This is about fields that will disappear if you coast right now.

If you're sticking with the road to awesome, you're going to work the hardest you've ever worked in the land of Harvesting.

## THE HARVEST ROOSTER

One morning I woke up at 4:00 a.m. in Indianapolis.

I wasn't there to work out for the Colts, but that's a pretty good assumption given the cannon I call my right arm.

I was in a hotel, waking up after speaking the night before in Grant County, Indiana. Grant County is sixty miles and seven circles away from Indianapolis. Most maps don't factor in the circles, but they should if you get the same cab I did. The driver and I could see the hotel glowing in the midnight darkness. We could almost touch it, we were so close to that Holiday Inn Express. But the driver couldn't find the entrance. So we circled the building a few times like a shark assessing its prey.

We finally found the driveway, and I checked in at 12:30 a.m. Roughly three hours later I was up for a flight to San Antonio to speak.

Before I took a few tentative steps into the land of Harvesting, I didn't expect so many 4 a.m. alarm clocks. I bought into the myth that when you find your awesome, things will be easy. Life will flow like a gentle river of Fresca, passing banks of Twizzler grass. There's a melon-colored ribbon you twirl. La. La. La.

I was wrong. Here's the truth:

You will work harder at something you love than at something you like.

You will work harder than you have ever worked when you start chasing a dream.

You will hustle and grind and sweat and push and pull.

You will get up earlier and go to bed later. But that's okay.

Know why?

Joy is an incredible alarm clock.

It will wake you up and keep you up and pick you up and gently pull you through a thousand rejections along the way.

If your goal is to work less, stay on the road to average. Do something you just kind of like. Settle into life like a long winter's nap and coast on through to your 80s.

But if you want to dream—if you want to live out some unique talent you've been given to steward during your time on this planet—get used to 4 a.m. alarms.

Get going.

Get up.

Continue Harvesting.

## THE CROP CIRCLES OF SUPPORT

Don't become a jerk. Don't get lazy. Don't get entitled.

Easier said than done. How do you avoid the surprising number of traps that spring up in the land of Harvesting? You don't face them alone. You spend some time cultivating the crop circles of support.

And like everything else in this book, they're not complicated. In fact, there are only three circles of support you need to think about as you continue down the road to awesome.

The level of support you need is highest in the center and lowest on the edges, which is why we're going to start right there.

### Inner Circle: Spouse

The absolute worst place you can put your spouse is on the opposite side of your dream. When that happens, the harder you lean into your awesome, the farther you push your spouse away. Without even realizing how you got to such different places, you start saying things like, "Don't you want me to pursue my dream? Is that it? Your dream is for me to be unhappy? Con-grats, then—you're already living your dream!"

Cue plate toss, and not the fun kind like the Greeks do in rings of fire at festivals.

Is that an exaggeration? Maybe slightly, but it's not far off from a reality that happens every single day. The truth is that if you're married, awesome is a team sport. Traveling your road to awesome with your spouse is twice as fun as being on it by yourself.

What are the two things you need to do right now if you're married and trying to be awesome?

## Make action payments

Words are so cheap when it comes to dreaming. And yet, most of us, when confronted with the challenge of getting a spouse to support our dream, run right back to words. We believe that perhaps the first ten million we offered just weren't the right ones. Maybe the next ten million will do the trick. So we talk and we talk and we talk about what we're going to do with our awesome. And we exhaust our spouses.

Do you know what's better than words? Action. Actions always beat words. Action always beats intention. What you've done is always more powerful than what you're going to do.

Want a spouse to support you? Get up thirty minutes before the rest of the house wakes up and work on your dream. Turn off the TV and read twenty pages of a book by an expert in the field you're pursuing. Take a second job to raise the startup money your dream might take instead of draining your savings account.

Make action payments if you want to get your spouse to believe you're serious about the pursuit of awesome. Because chances are, this isn't the first time you've flirted with a dream. This is probably the thirty-seventh time, and the minute you start with a new one, all those words and all those intentions you never followed through on are going to burst into your spouse's memory.

Erase them with action payments. And they have to be drawn out of your account, not hers or his. You don't gain any support if you sacrifice your spouse's time for your dream. It has to be your time. If you come home and say, "In order to show you how important this dream is to me, I'm going to cancel our date night," you won't go deeper into the land of Harvesting. You'll go deeper into the land of couch sleeping.

This simple idea is one of the biggest reasons my wife, Jenny, was able to jump on board with the move to Nashville from Atlanta. I'd compiled a history of action payments. I'd made a million other big plans that never went anywhere. But for two years she saw me get up early to write. She saw me say no to a lot of fun things I may have liked to do in order to say yes to the things I felt called to do. She knew I was serious about this. Not because of my words—those are cheap and untrustworthy. But because of my actions, which are expensive and trustworthy.

## Master how versus wow

I didn't come up with this, but I wish I had, because it's brilliant. A guy named John Woodall in Atlanta once told an audience I was in that in every marriage there are two types of people: a "How" person and a "Wow" person.

The Wow person tends to be the dreamer. They come up with big ideas and big dreams and big wild plans. They bounce off the walls with what might be.

The How person tends to be the strategist. They want the details and the steps and the logistics of any given situation.

They're both great approaches to life, but when they bump together, disaster can occur.[3]

The Wow person says, "I've got a great idea. What if we sold our house and invested all the money into an artisanal pickle stand in the hipster section of town? We could wrap each pickle in a napkin with prose written on it. We'll call it 'Pickles & Poems.' It will be huge!"

The How person, wanting to show the Wow person love, offers up their greatest strength, a series of How questions. "How would we make money with that? How would we have health insurance? How many licenses would we need to sell street pickles? How would we print the napkins? How would we outfit a van or a car for pickle distribution?"

Those are all very legitimate questions, only the Wow person doesn't hear them that way. The Wow person hears an attack. And they attack back.

Then the two storm off and don't dream together that day.

If you stack enough of those conversations on top of each other, the Wow person eventually stops sharing his or her dreams. It's not that they stop dreaming, they just stop sharing them with the How spouse. Those dreams go somewhere, often to someone online who "gets me." That's how a lot of emotional affairs begin and part of the reason the word *Facebook* showed up on a third of all divorce filings in 2011.[4]

To prevent this from happening in my own marriage—because that's where we were headed with me (the Wow person) and my wife (the How person)—we took Woodall's advice and started to do two things.

### Two weeks of wow

When I first discuss a new Wow idea with my wife, do you know what she says? "Wow." She doesn't ask How questions. She doesn't list the myriad of details she'd love to know. She simply gives me the gift of Wow. What she trusts is that, more than likely, I'm not going to do anything with this idea. In two weeks, or more realistically, two hours, I will have moved on to something else. So for the first two weeks, I get a grace period of Wow. We just bounce the idea around without ever worrying about a How making a cameo in the conversation. If after two weeks I'm still passionate about the idea, Jenny jumps in with some great Hows. She's a genius, and I am so blessed to be married to her. Her ability to provide shape to the Wows I bring up is unbelievable. As she once said to me, "We should work together more. Together we make one pretty amazing person." Instead of a How/Wow blow-up, we get to turn our differences into strengths, not weaknesses.

### Wow disclaimer

The first thing I say to my wife when I talk with her about a Wow idea is, "I'm not about to sell our house. I'm not thinking about emptying our savings account." I offer the Wow disclaimer. It turns out that my wife is a fan of stability and security. She digs both of those things. Who knew? It took counseling to wake me up to what was going on when I spouted off dreams *at* Jenny instead of *with* Jenny. At one point, our counselor said, "Jon and Jenny, you both have tremendous insight into Jon." That was his polite way of saying, "Jon, shut up! You're filling the entire relationship with you and not thinking at all about Jenny's perspective." So in addition to learning to listen, I had to learn to talk too. And part of that meant being up-front about the Wows I was excited about. It's amazing what a two-sentence disclaimer can do to defuse a situation. Knowing that I'm not about to launch out on some financially fatal adventure (like the ad agency I started) sets Jenny at ease. Always disclaim your dreams if you're married to a How person.

## Middle Circle: Friends and Family

Did you stop chasing awesome because you're not married yet and feel like without a spouse it's impossible?

Good, that's exactly what I was trying to communicate. I'm glad it came across so clearly.

If you're not married, your middle circle becomes your inner circle. The rings just shift in one, as a best friend or a family member becomes your greatest source of support. The question I most often get, though, when it comes to the middle circle is this: "What do I do if no one supports my dream?"

Maybe that's your story right now. Your family members, your friends, your coworkers—no one gets on board with what you feel you're called to do. You explain it to them and share it with as much enthusiasm and clarity as you can possibly muster. But still, nobody is willing to support your dream.

Or maybe you've got a little support from friends and family, but you'd love a lot more.

In either situation, the next steps are the same. You have to give people in the middle circle patience and support.

## Patience

Awesome is a little weird. You've probably already figured that out. I mean, we entered a forest of voices and explored a diamond mine. That's a little strange. Those kinds of things don't tend to happen on the road to average. And that's the problem. People understand average.

We all get how average works. We're immersed in a world of average every day. If you tell friends and family members, "I'm going to stay average," they may wonder why you felt the need to say that out loud, but they'll never call you crazy.

No one pursuing a life of average ever received a dire warning of failure from a family member. No one pursuing a life of average ever left a Thanksgiving dinner feeling like everyone criticized their pursuit. No one pursuing a life of average was ever made fun of by other average people.

But if you decide to travel the road to awesome, you will be.

Family members and friends will not understand your dream. The natural response will be to either change your tactics of communication or lash out. In the first approach, you try for the one millionth time to get Dad to understand your dream 100 percent. In the second, you interpret the lack of understanding as an attack and return the favor. Neither way is that fun or effective.

Instead of reacting that way when someone doesn't understand your dream, give them the gift of patience. The reality is that they shouldn't understand your dream 100 percent. If they did, it wouldn't be your dream—it'd be their dream. They'd be the one chasing it, not you.

You're the one who has taken a thousand steps down the road to awesome. You're the one who has had all the experiences. It would be impossible for someone else to understand your dream without having that same journey.

We understand this when it comes to other types of trips we take in life.

For example, my little sister, Molly, spent five months in Seville, Spain. While there, she ran a marathon in Madrid. The summer after the experience, she spent a few weeks at our house in Nashville. She told the most amazing stories. She showed us beautiful photos, gave my kids souvenirs, and unraveled the five months for us.

Which made me an expert on what it feels like to live in Seville, Spain.

I totally understood everything that happened there. On the third night she stayed with us, I stood up, put my hand on Molly's shoulder, and told her, "Let me stop you right there. I've got it. I 100 percent understand what it feels like to live in Spain as an American. I've never taken a single step in Madrid, but I know what it's like to run a marathon there. You don't have to tell me anything else. I understand."

If I had told her that, my wife would have leg-swept me and probably made me sleep under the couch in our living room. That would have been an idiotic thing to say, because it's impossible.

I've never been to Spain. How could I ever think that I can perfectly understand what that experience was like for my sister? And that was only five months of her living there. How can we carry dreams in our heart for years, maybe even decades, and then expect our friends and family members to understand them perfectly?

They won't.

Don't be surprised by that.

Don't be devastated by that.

Don't think it's because you've failed to explain it the right way.

There's going to be some degree of disconnect. It's your dream, not theirs.

Give them the gift of patience. Give them time to understand your dream.

## Support

One of the best things you can do to get support for your dream is to support somebody else's first. When you run into a wall of resistance or indifference from friends and family members, stop asking, "How can I get them to be a fan of my dream?" and instead ask, "How can I be a fan of their dream?"

Tell the mom who doesn't get what you're trying to do, "I've explained my dream a few times, but I've never asked you, what's yours?" Tell the friend who is having a hard time understanding what you're trying to do, "You know what I'm passionate about, but what's something that you're passionate about?" Tell the boyfriend who may think you're a little crazy, "I feel like I've bumped into something I'm designed to do, but what about you? Is there something you feel that way about? Is there a way I can help you pursue that?"

Asking these questions may be awkward at first because nobody usually asks them. We usually don't take interest in other people's hearts and hopes. We stay surface level with so many different relationships that sometimes it feels weird to ask what someone is passionate about. But that's okay, because there is great kindness in asking someone what their dream is.

If you want help for your dream, start by helping someone else with their dream. If you want support for your hope, start by giving support to someone else's hope. If you want encouragement as you work on your calling, start by encouraging other people.

Giving support is often the best way to get it.

## Outer Circle: Fellow Travelers

The outer support circle is fellow travelers, people who are on their own roads to awesome. They can challenge you, motivate you, and celebrate with you.

## Challenge

On Wednesdays, I have breakfast with a group of guys in Nashville. When I moved to the city, I put the group together because I knew how dangerous the road to awesome could be if you walk it alone.

One morning I was telling the guys about a tweetup I had. If you've never been to one, then congratulations; you haven't had to use that horrible word. A tweetup is where you meet with people you know from Twitter. I held my first one in Oklahoma City and told the guys that we had sixty people.

Almost under my breath I said, "But I would have been happy with ten!"

My friend Chris Thomas immediately said, "Really? Would you have been happy with ten?"

I paused dramatically, something I'm always doing in stories I retell, and said, "No, I wouldn't have. I actually wanted 100. I'm not that happy about sixty."

He laughed, I laughed, and then we threw a football in the parking lot to break the tension of that brief moment of intimacy.

He was right. I was lying so I'd look humble. I was starting to keep secret metrics and expectations on my road to awesome. And when Chris held up a mirror at breakfast, I got to see them for the first time. When he challenged me, I got to see the rocky road I was on and adjust my course.

## Motivation

You know you'll exercise more often if you have a workout partner. You won't be as likely to cheat on your diet or skip Pilates if you've got someone going through it with you. You'll get up early or forgo carbs if you know someone else is tracking with you.

If we understand the benefit of having a workout partner, how come we don't replicate that same thing in other parts of our lives?

Why wouldn't you have a dream partner? Probably because the phrase "dream partner" is pretty lame. But other than that, it's a concept you'd see instant results from in the form of motivation.

That's why my friend Stephen calls me regularly and says, "Be Jay-Z." He's using a little shorthand we've developed in the last two years. He's motivating me to be driven and focused and hardworking. After watching Jay-Z methodically build an empire, he's motivating me to do the same—save for the marriage to Beyoncé and incredibly crisp billed hats.

Is that silly? A little, but it is no less silly than having someone yell, "You got this! Give me three more!" in a gym and expecting results. That person is probably even in tight clothing and sweaty at the time. That's sillier. But it works, doesn't it? Motivation from fellow travelers—whether in the gym or on the road to awesome—is a powerful thing.

## Celebration

My friend Brewster and I invented a table.

I know what you're thinking right now: *Of course you did. I've seen your photo in this book. Your callus-free writer hands may say* IKEA, *but your picture indicates that you're burly and rugged and clearly know your way around a bandsaw.*

While I appreciate you noticing all those things, it's not that kind of table. It's not made of wood. It has no legs and can only hold one thing, but I promise you it's a table that everyone needs.

What is it?

A brag table.

Brewster and I created it after having breakfast for a few weeks. We'd been trying to become better friends and encourage each other, but we realized we were being a little dishonest. Every week we'd edit the things we were proud of or excited about because we didn't want to appear cocky or arrogant. We'd paint our weeks with a bit of false humility and share them with each other.

But eventually we realized that's really dumb.

Excitement isn't the same thing as arrogance.

Talking about a project you knocked out of the park doesn't mean you're cocky.

Celebrating some accomplishment or goal doesn't make you a jerk.

We decided that everywhere else in life we may need to be quiet. We may need to downplay things or stand behind the scenes, but at the brag table we would cheer as loudly as we wanted for our dreams and each other. We refused to believe that your only two options as a young leader are to be a cocky jerk or to never openly discuss something you're proud of.

We decided to create a third option—a middle ground. We call it the brag table.

There, at breakfast, we celebrate each other and share our triumphs without the fear of someone saying, "That's a humble brag," or "Get over yourself." Being vulnerable about your failures is only half of the story; you have to be vulnerable enough to share your successes too.

Which is why I loved getting a text from Brewster one day. It said, "Can I approach the brag table?" I said, "Of course!" And then we got to cheer over text about an award he had recently won. The brag table went virtual!

If you're in the land of Harvesting, be honest. Don't pretend that being excited about the crop you're seeing in this land is the same exact thing as being arrogant. It's not. You're going to need your own brag table.

## DON'T CHASE MORE INSTEAD OF AWESOME

One day I had two conversations with two very different friends. One was 26 and a business owner from California. One was 58 and an author from Tennessee. On the outside, they didn't have a lot in common. But they were both having the same problem, and it's one you'll face in the land of Harvesting.

When crops pop up in your life, people are going to rush to your side and say, "More!" They will tell you that you could harvest more or grow more or benefit more if you'd just increase production. If you expanded the territory, you'd triple or quadruple your awesome. And they may be right—maybe you could harvest more if you'd just do these few additional things. But when someone tells you, "More!" I want you to ask them, "Why?"

My young friend in California didn't at first. His company was blowing up. He made $500,000 in one week. I don't know your salary at 26, but I'm almost positive I didn't get paid $2 million a month. In the midst of that growth, people were coming out of the woodwork to tell him, "More!" That his harvest was nothing compared to what it could be. If he'd just push a little harder, try a little harder, expand here and grow there, things could be even bigger. He'd have more.

He took the advice for a while, and the only "more" he ended up with was more exhausted. He ended up taking ten days off from the company in the middle of the swirl because he realized he didn't have any Central Park.

Meanwhile, on the other side of the country, my friend in Tennessee had just released a new book. He was in a fun scene of Harvesting. A young entrepreneur found out about it and asked him to lunch. Over the meal, he laid out an extensive plan to grow my friend's book and platform. My friend had a good start, but it could be so much more. If he'd just do the right things on Twitter and social media and maybe travel more, he'd be able to really blow up his book. He'd get more.

Instead of agreeing to the proposal, my friend said what I want you to say in moments like that: "Why?"

"Why do I need to do that? I like my book. I'm proud of the book, and I've got twenty years to sell it and grow it. If I follow your proposal, it will be really hard for me to maintain my day job, which I love, or be a good husband or dad. Why do I need more right this second?"

The entrepreneur was stunned. No one asks why to "More!" They just chase it. And strain for it. And often wind up with a whole lot of stuff they never really wanted in the first place— someone else's idea of awesome, but not their own.

People are going to tell you, "More!" in the land of Harvesting. When they do, ask them, "Why?" And if they don't have an answer that suits your version of awesome, don't change a thing.

## DON'T CHASE ACCOMPLISHMENTS INSTEAD OF AWESOME

Eventually, fourteen people are going to come to your breakout session. That's what happened to me twenty-four hours ago in Pasadena, California.

I was scheduled to give a keynote to about 450 people at a conference on a Tuesday night. But first, I would do a breakout session in the afternoon.

I don't know what number of people I assumed would attend my breakout, but it was more than fourteen.

After giving people a few extra minutes to come in, I started the session. It was brutal. For one thing, nobody ever sits together in situations like that. The room was massive, with seating for probably 300 people, and there were only fourteen people there. And people don't laugh when they're spread out and sitting by themselves.

Normally in situations like that you're supposed to ask people to move up and sit together, but I was so caught off guard by the low attendance that I became flustered. Part of the reason I was thrown off was that I could hear the laughter through the wall from the breakout next to mine. There were hundreds of people attending that breakout, and the awesomeness they were all experiencing kept washing over into my sad little room. Right as I would try to make a point, a new crescendo of applause and laughter would erupt, and I'd hang my head for a second while it finished.

What was supposed to be a seventy-five-minute speech turned into a forty-five-minute speech. As I was packing up to leave, three people came in late and were surprised it was over already. I decided to stay and do the whole thing over for them.

Overall, it was a rough day, made rougher by the three-month winning streak I had been on. My last five events had been to crowds of 5,000 to 10,000 people. I was starting to focus on my accomplishments. Look at me! Big speaker guy!

Suddenly, the rug was pulled out from under me. It wouldn't have been so bad if I could have retreated. If I could have gotten back on a Southwest flight home, pretended a bag of peanuts was enough of a meal for a cross-country flight, and then punched an indie musician in the Nashville airport. But I couldn't do that.

Three hours after my bomb of a breakout, I had to do my keynote. I had to get back up onstage in the main ballroom and speak to the entire conference.

As I walked back to the hotel to change shirts, I thought about what a lousy fuel accomplishments make. Not that they're not fun. Not that they're not to be celebrated or shared at the brag table. Not that you shouldn't aim for them, but just that they can't be your chief motivation. They can't be why you do what you do. They can't be the gas that powers you down the road to awesome. Because one day, in the middle of Harvesting, some situation is going to fall apart.

You'll be expecting 100 people to show up for your event, and fourteen will come. You'll be expecting some video you did to go viral, and it won't. You'll be expecting to sell 1,000 copies of your book, and you won't. And you won't have time to find a new accomplishment to charge you back up.

You'll have to take another step, start another job, get back up onstage, and pretend you're not talking to 436 people who chose not to go to your breakout three hours earlier. Because guess what? It's time to start being awesome. Whether you had 2 or 2,000 people at your store opening, it's time be awesome the next day. And the day after that.

You have to love the act of being awesome.

Writing, selling, singing, running a business—whatever the act is, that's what has to fuel you through the land of Harvesting.

Even if you harvest a thousand accomplishments during your time in this land, treat them as rewards for what you do, not the reasons for what you do.

## FEAR NOT THE HARVEST

The fear of failure, though widely discussed and understood, is grossly overrated. It is not the scariest fear there is. Far scarier and far more surprising when it hits you in the land of Harvesting is the fear of success.

Even that phrase feels a little ridiculous: "Fear of success." That doesn't make any sense. Isn't that what we've been striving for all these weeks or months or years? Wasn't that always the goal? Now that it finally starts happening in the land of Harvesting, how can we possibly be afraid of it?

In 1915, Sigmund Freud tried to answer those questions in an essay titled "Those Wrecked by Success." In it, he theorized about the "surprising and even bewildering" tendency of some people to fall apart "precisely when a deeply rooted and long-cherished wish has come to fulfillment . . . as though they were not able to tolerate happiness."

What a terrible trap that is, desperate to achieve something but then quick to destroy it when it occurs.

Elissa Sklaroff, a Philadelphia therapist who treats success-fearing executives, continues this line of thinking. "Being on the brink of success brings a crisis," she wrote, "and all of our neuroses pop right up to the surface. On some level, success-fearing people are running from change—especially from having to change their secret self-image as an unsuccessful or undeserving person."[5]

Turns out our secret selves, the ones we each decided we needed to be at the start of this book, are undeserving and unsuccessful.

That's how I feel some days. It comes down to history. For thirty years, I was a mess-up. I know how to be a mess-up, and nobody expects anything from the mess-up. All you're expected to do is mess up. Failure becomes more than just an event; it becomes your identity. Average becomes your address. When my first book came out and people started to ask me to speak at different places, it was a little terrifying. The hero's clothes weighed more than the villain's or the victim's clothes to me. I know how to play those roles. I know how to fail and feel sorry for myself. Fear and doubt will try to encourage you to believe you are still the victim or the villain, because they are terrified you will make it to the land of Guiding and help other people down their own roads. But if you think you're the villain or the victim, you won't help others. Victims don't guide. And villains? They spread hurt, not hope.

Success was new and uncharted and ill-fitting to me. I found myself often wanting to slip right back to average where I'd spent all those years before. It was more like home to me than awesome. If you spend too long anywhere, it becomes what you are used to.

For some of you, this will not make any sense. I am glad for that. Perhaps you know the truth of who you really are, and failure is not an identity you ever accepted. But for others, you are feeling a little homesick in the land of Harvesting.

Sometimes we're afraid of success because if one area of our lives gets awesome, it will force us to deal with the area we're really afraid of. We will look for any distraction from the issue we really don't want to deal with. If we can wreck our success, we'll still have something to focus on that can save us from seeing what's really hurting us. It can save us from starting again on something else.

There's a powerful example of this very issue in the movie *Buck*. *Buck* is a documentary about Buck Brannaman, the man *The Horse Whisperer* is loosely based on. As a child, Buck and his brother were rodeo stars with a hard-driving father. Celebrated around the nation for their roping skills, Buck and his brother seemed to have the perfect life. Off camera, though, their father beat them mercilessly. Eventually, a coach at school saw the bruises on Buck and his brother and promised them he'd make sure no one would ever do that to them again. Years later Buck became famous in horse circles for his unbelievable way to train a horse without ever resorting to violence.

It's an amazing documentary full of great truth, but the most interesting moment is when a woman brings an incredibly dangerous horse to Buck to train. The stallion is out of control, kicking violently, and eventually bites Buck's coworker in the head, causing a deep gash.

Buck talks with the owner and asks her about the stallion. She says that he is one of eighteen stallions that live on her farm. Incredulous that the woman would have more than one stallion on her property, Buck cuts right to the chase:

You're nuts for having that many studs running together, lady, I'm telling you that. Most people don't need studs, and they don't need eighteen of them. I don't know what you're trying to prove. And if you've got a lot going on in your life, probably a lot of it is a lot bigger story than this horse. You ought to be a SEAL team member or something as much risk as you like to take. Why don't you learn how to enjoy your life? Life is too short. This horse tells me quite a bit about you. This is just an amplified situation of what is. Maybe there's some things for you to learn about you.

She breaks down, and you get the sense that this was never about the horse. This was about some other hurt. Some part of her life that was so raw and unsettled that the only way to ignore it was to make a different part of life even crazier. If she had sold those stallions, established a successful farm, and put out that particular fire in her house, she'd be forced to admit there was an elephant in the room. Later in the film, she cries in her interview and says, "He's right. I mean, he's right. I . . . you know? He's right. It's not just the horse. He's right about my life."[6]

The chaos of the horses was the perfect hiding place from some other part of her life. Success with the stallions—essentially an impossibility—would have uncovered her hiding place.

That's the same reason I threw a tantrum over a hyphen.

My book *Quitter* was about to come out. Speaking engagements were picking up. Opportunities were multiplying, and it felt like I was walking into a season of Harvesting. I instinctually tried to pump the brakes and throw a monkey wrench into the process. I started freaking out about whether or not the cover should have a hyphen in the word *best-selling*. I took pictures of books at airports and texted them to my team members. I emailed people about my concerns and tried to dig my heels in for a long, drawn-out battle over the hyphen.

I didn't want the book to come out. I was afraid of the success and bent on trying to slow things down. And rather than deal with my issues that the book release was exposing—secretly believing I was meant to be a failure—I clung with everything I had to a hyphen.

Fortunately, no one took my bait. They refused to believe my protests that the hyphen decision would significantly impact the number of books we sold. The book came out. And I had to face some things I'd been running from for years.

It was easier to hide when I was working at a job I didn't love and not chasing my awesome. I could say things like, "Someday I'll write a book. Someday I'll speak. Someday I'll pursue all these dreams." Until that day came, I could ignore all the other issues in my life. I had a target for my distraction. But once I had written a book and done a few speaking gigs and experienced a little bit of success, there was suddenly space in my life. In the land of Harvesting, you'll find that there's room and an invitation to keep exploring who you are and who you were meant to be. That can be scary. But don't run from it. Don't fear the harvest. And don't fight it. Lean into it and know that in many ways, your adventure in awesome is just beginning. That's because every harvest ushers in a new start.

# GUIDING

**A FRIEND ONCE TOLD ME** that every great story has the same four parts:

**Innocence**
**Innocence lost**
**Coping with the loss**
**Resolution**

He then proceeded to show me how every successful movie follows that pattern. Take *Toy Story 3,* for instance. In the first scene, the toys are being played with—their definition of innocence. Then their owner, Andy, goes to college, and they find themselves discarded in a trash bag—innocence lost. Then they make it to a day care, but there's a villain there they must cope with. The movie eventually concludes with the toys living with a new little kid who will play with them like Andy used to do—resolution.

I think that breakdown works perfectly for movies and sit-coms because eventually the credits roll. The lights come back on, the audience goes home, and the story is over. But ours isn't. Unless they are reading this book out loud at your graveside service, your story has many scenes left. But if you're not careful, if you think fear is done trying to quietly seduce you back to average, you'll get stuck firmly in the land of Guiding. You'll buy the lie that one trip down the road to awesome was enough. You may even think that one harvest was all you are capable of. You'd be wrong.

## HOW TO TURN A HEADLINE INTO AN EPITAPH

As I've already mentioned, in November 2009, the readers of my blog helped raise $60,000 to build two kindergartens in Vietnam.

My favorite part of that story is how quickly they raised the first $30,000. If you remember, 2009 wasn't the greatest year for our economy. Houses were selling for a nickel, the mortgage industry was imploding, and unemployment was ramping up. Into that landscape we dared attempt to raise an initial $30,000 for a village no one had heard of, in a country most of us would never have the chance to visit.

We thought the project would take weeks to complete. Do you know how long it took? Eighteen hours! The entire $30,000 was raised in less than a day. If you didn't read my blog that Monday, you missed it. (That's why we decided to raised another $30,000 and build a second kindergarten.)

It was a fun moment that made for a great headline in the *Atlanta Journal-Constitution*: "Blogger raises $30,000 in 18 hours."

But three years later I had turned that headline into an epitaph on a gravestone in the land of Guiding.

I didn't intend to get stuck in the land of Guiding, but nobody ever warned me that the story pattern my friend shared is, in real life, incomplete. Nobody told me that after "Resolution" comes "Start a new story."

So instead of starting again, I got really comfortable in the land of Guiding. I told the story about our fundraiser dozens of times to dozens of audiences. I knew just which parts to drag out dramatically. I had just the right amount of jokes peppered throughout so it never got too heavy. And then I'd ask the crowd, "Do you know how long it took us to raise the money?" Then I'd pause perfectly and let the tension build before yelling, "Eighteen hours!" (Only once did someone in the crowd actually answer my question by guessing, "Three hours!" before I could reveal the real number. Me then saying, "Eighteen hours" after his impossibly optimistic guess of three hours was a bit of a letdown.)

It was a wonderful story, and with each passing week and month and year, it became firmly ingrained into who I thought I was.

I didn't even notice that was happening until it came time to tell a new story. My wife and I wanted to do another project. We'd done small ones in the years between but had never jumped back into another big project. One night I told my wife that I was ready. I was ready to start again. I was ready to raise $25,000!

When I told her that, it got a little quiet in the living room. I think she was mentally doing the math in her head. *Okay, first project raised $60,000. Next project, we're going to really stretch* *ourselves and raise $25,000!* After a few seconds, she spoke up. In her succinct style that has caused many a reader to say, "When will your wife write a book already?" she said to me, "I dare you to lose some face."

Oh, Bryan Adams, love does cut like a knife! She had me. I didn't decide to raise $25,000 because that's what I felt called to do or that's the number the charity organization needed. I picked $25,000 because I was afraid I'd fail to raise as much as last time and in the process kill the headline I'd turned into a myth and, ultimately, my epitaph. I picked $25,000 because I thought we would easily eclipse that and I'd get a new headline: "Blogger raises $25,000 in 4 hours!" Hooray for me! Can we pause here for a second and review the depths of my ridiculousness? I was basing this new project to build a hospital in Vietnam on its ability to protect my ego. I don't know what you did today that was dastardly, but surely it's not as bad as that. At the bare minimum, you should feel better about your own life while reading this book.

Realizing what I was doing with the $25,000 project, my wife and I decided to regroup and figure out new ways we could partner with organizations to do even bigger projects in the future.

How did I get stuck in the land of Guiding, though? How did I take eighteen months to learn, edit, master, and harvest an idea like building an online community that raises money, only to fall right back into average when it was all said and done?

Fear and doubt.

Though we've punched those enemies in the face a thousand times throughout our journey, they refuse to give us a free pass in any land, especially the last one.

But at least they are consistent; at least we know what they are going to tell us in the land of Guiding. At least we won't be surprised when they attempt to argue both sides of the coin.

## THE STARTING CYCLE

My friend John Crist is a comedian. He's toured internationally, opened up for some big names, and has a lot of the pieces necessary for a long career in place. But he still bombs. He still has nights where the laughs are few and the heckles are plentiful. One night in the middle of his set, he told the crowd, "I care about the environment; that's why the chain saw I use to cut down so many trees is solar-powered." A woman in the crowd stopped the entire show by launching into a loud monologue about the impossibility of a solar-powered chain saw. Turns out she came from a family of loggers.

As you watch John lose the crowd on the video of that night, his face seems to say, "Really? Of all the impossible scenarios I've shared tonight in the form of jokes, it's the solar-powered chain saw that is going to wreck this moment?"

How do you prepare for the possibility of a lumberjack's aggressive daughter in the audience? You don't. So on some nights, John bombs. That's part of comedy, and when we talked about it one day on the phone, I realized it was part of Guiding too.

John told me that the best part of comedy was that he didn't have to carry around the failures for that long. I asked him what he meant. He explained:

A failure would hurt a lot if I were only performing once a month or once every other month. There'd be a thirty- to sixty-day window for me to carry around that failure. I'd sit with it for all those weeks and it'd be really heavy. But with comedy, if I fail during the 7:00 p.m. show, I only have to carry it for an hour until the 8:00 p.m. show. It doesn't have time to define me when I start again so quickly.

John learned that if he can shorten his starting cycle, failures don't have the time to define him. At the end of the night, what happened at 7:00 p.m. doesn't hold a whole lot of weight when he performed successfully at 8:00 p.m. and 9:00 p.m. He starts so often that the shadow of one failure looks tiny in the light of all the new opportunities for success.

The same principle applies with success. If you don't start again, if you don't share what you've learned with other travelers and head back to the land of Learning with a fresh start, yesterday's successes will start to define your today and tomorrow. Instead of just celebrating them, which you should do, you'll start to protect them—to manicure the myth. And you'll be afraid to start over for fear of losing your successful identity. That's why I got stuck in the land of Guiding. I didn't start again quickly enough because I was fearful of losing my successful identity.

That's the brilliance of fear and doubt. If your first stroll down the road to awesome didn't generate the results you expected, they will tell you, "See, we told you this whole thing was a waste of time. You failed! Average is where you belong."

On the other hand, if you do experience some success and make it to the land of Guiding, fear and doubt will whisper, "Don't leave. What if this was just a lucky break? What if your new next adventure isn't as successful as this one? What if you can't maintain this momentum? Don't try again."

That's what happened to another friend of mine. She signed a two-book publishing deal. She made it to the land of Guiding and even helped me with some advice when I was getting started. But she never made it back out herself. Her first book came out in 1995. She told me a wonderful idea for the second book in 2001. It's now more than a decade later, and there is no second book in sight.

The true tragedy of a "one-hit wonder" isn't that someone releases one big song and then never has another song that is popular. They're still making music in that scenario; they just didn't sell a lot of copies. They're still living out of their definition of awesome. They're still sharing their gift.

The real tragedy of a one-hit wonder is when someone succeeds once and then never tries again.

No matter your circumstances, if you want to be more awesome, you've got to start again. That begins in the land of Guiding when you start helping others down the paths they're on. It continues when you return to the land of Learning with something new of your own to start. Though it may look large at first, the gap between the land of Guiding and the land of Learning is surprisingly small.

## THE BORDERLESS LANDS BEYOND

"I've got a challenge I need your help with."

That was the email that brought me down to Dave Ramsey's office seventy-two hours before his new book tour kicked off. He hadn't written a new book in seven years. He would visit more than twenty cities in thirty days. He would fly around the country and speak to tens of thousands of people. Our entire company was coiled tightly, like a spring ready for the massive launch.

And the challenge Dave had in that moment had nothing to do with the book.

"The reason we do all of this is for the people out there who need hope. During the book tour, I'd love to hear everyone's story and spend time with them, but if I do that, I won't be able to serve the people at the back of the line. With 2,000 people per event, how do I let everyone there know that their story matters to us?"

On the edge of a project years in the making, when a lot of leaders would be asking, "How do I get these folks through the line faster?" Dave was asking, "How do I serve them better?" He was asking, "How do I make sure that the woman in Ohio, who just lost her house and is in tears, knows that we're here to help her?"

This wasn't something he was doing for the stage or a camera or any sort of publicity. This was him and me alone in his office, talking about the final land on the road to awesome—Guiding.

The secret that Dave knows and the one that took me years to understand is this: helping other people better their lives is way more fun than obsessing about bettering your own.

Awesome always goes viral.

Joy is contagious.

When you find something you love doing, you can't help but want to tell other people how to find something they love doing too. When the memory fog of average has cleared from your head and the true availability of awesome has been revealed, you want everyone to know. That is the progression of awesome 100 percent of the time.

No one ever uses their new lease on life to make sure other people's lives are more miserable. Ebenezer Scrooge sprinted through the snowy town when he was given a second chance on life. In *It's a Wonderful Life*, George Bailey ran through the streets when he was given a second chance at life. If the saying "Hurt people hurt people" is true—and I believe it is—then the opposite is true as well. "Helped people help people."

You may not be a teacher. You may not think you're a leader. You may have been selfish your entire life leading up to your first step on the road to awesome (I was). But upon enjoying the fruits of your first harvest and then crossing into the land of Guiding, you'll start to feel the rumble of the question, "How do I help other people do this?"

To answer that question, you'll first have to put to bed three Guiding myths. That phrase sounds a little like the name of a soap opera that combines the issues of a modern dynasty based in New Jersey with the problems of the ancient Greeks in years gone by. *Guiding Myths: Where Socrates Meets Seacaucus.* Guiding, fortunately, will not be that dramatic, and in most cases, it tends to sneak up on you. Though you may not have known it, you've been guiding since the moment you took your first step on the road to awesome. Because all it takes to guide is to be one step ahead of someone else.

When you were in the land of Learning, friends who were still stuck on average were watching you. You guided them even if not on purpose. When you were in the land of Editing, family members who were behind you in the land of Learning were monitoring your progress. Some were being inspired by your progress. When you were in Mastering . . . I think you know where I'm going with this. We've got five lands—this could take forever.

I personally don't have a great track record when it comes to guiding. My low point was probably when I got caught shoplifting on the way to a church youth group leader's meeting in the ninth grade (I had a smidge of what you might call "hypocrisy" in my life). That phone call from the police station was not a fun one for me or my father, the pastor. Since then, though, I have learned how to move beyond the three myths that tend to cripple most people in the land of Guiding.

## Myth #1: You shouldn't guide until you feel ready.

One day I met a visual artist who wanted to work on some new projects. He told me, "I want to help people in Christian filmmaking, but I don't have any experience in that." I asked him what he was currently doing. He replied, "I did a lot of the motion graphics for the *Transformer* movies and currently own a design company with about fifty employees." I tried to suppress a small giggle. "*Transformers*? You worked on the motion graphics for *Transformers* and don't feel like you've got the experience you need to break into the motion graphic scene within Christian filmmaking?"

I immediately called my friend Scott, who runs the ECHO conference in Dallas, and within a matter of days my new friend Sean was scheduled to lead a breakout. Why didn't Sean see how qualified and ready he was to guide other people?

Because no one can see that about themselves. The talent we have the hardest time recognizing is our own. As author Derek Sivers says, the way you look at the world is "obvious to you" but often "amazing to others."[1] You can't see it because you've seen it for years, if not your whole life. But for other people? Your awesome is fresh and new and worthy of being shared. Don't feel ready to guide? That's okay; nobody does. Guide anyway.

## Myth #2: You should only share your successes.

Sometimes I fail. And when I do, I say these four words: "This too shall post." It used to be "This too shall pass," but then I learned something about sharing my failures with readers of my blog posts. People can relate to them. Chances are, they've had their own. Chances are, they thought they were the only ones. They can also learn from your experience. If you share honestly about your own failures, people can often avoid having the same thing happen to them. If you stepped in a hole and it hurt, it helps if you tell other people not to step in that same hole.

The temptation, of course, is to only share your success. From the stage as a public speaker or from the mailbox as a neighbor, it's much more comfortable to tell a story in which you made a wise decision. You look a little like a good guy. You win. Fight this temptation. We're full-up on guiders who only recount mistakes they made twenty years ago. We've got enough people on Facebook telling us about their perfect lives. We've got more celebrities crafting fictional reality lives than we can possibly stand. What we're missing is people who, when they fail, say, "This too shall post."

We need people who, instead of dramatizing the failure or glamorizing it or over-sharing in inappropriate ways, simply ask the question, "What did I learn in this experience that may help someone else?" You don't need a blog to "post" either. A post for you may mean coffee with a friend or a phone call to a family member. We all have the chance to post every day in a million different ways.

Now, don't take this to the extreme and believe the lie that "failure is the best way to learn." Guiding involves sharing both your failures *and* your successes. Success is actually the best way to learn. It's also the most fun way to learn. The problem is that you have to ask, "How?" after you succeed. How did that work? How did that succeed? How was that such a win? Success you improve on and share with other people is always a better teacher than failure.

Can failure teach great lessons? Without a doubt. But don't buy the romanticized version of failure our culture loves to shop around. Losing your only client is horrible. Losing your house is horrible. Getting fired is horrible. You'll definitely learn some lessons from those experiences, but having a successful business, having a successful job, and having a host of successful clients will teach you far more than failure ever will—if you'll stop to ask how and then share those results with the people you guide.

## Myth #3: Everyone should guide the exact same way.

For the last three years, I've had a monthly phone call with my friend Mike Foster. He's a few years ahead of me on the road to awesome and generously shares his wisdom in our regular hour-long phone calls. Around year two, I started to feel like maybe I needed to pay that forward. Maybe I needed to set up a few phone call meetings with guys younger than me and guide in the same way Mike guides me. My wife, who is smarter and half an inch taller than me, asked me the question I've asked you a lot in this book: "Why?"

"Why, do you think because he's guided you that way that you need to guide someone else that exact same way? You hate the phone. You're not that great at keeping appointments. Your ability to hold down a long-term work commitment over a period of years is spotty at best. Your strength is helping lots of people start. Play to that—don't just replicate what Mike is good at if you're not good at it too."

She was right. Sometimes in our desire to pay it forward, we think we have to pay it forward in the exact same way we received it. But Guiding, like every other land in this book, is not one-size-fits-all. Maybe a long-term, weekly coffee mentorship is how you need to guide someone. Maybe a blog where you share ideas you've learned is how you need to guide. Maybe a monthly discussion with a group of six guys is how you should guide. There are a million ways you can guide. Find the one that works best for you and then do that.

A lot.

## HOW TO GUIDE

The desire to help others is a natural by-product of being awesome. Being great at guiding is unfortunately not. Like every other land, Guiding takes discipline and wisdom.

If you've wrestled your way through the myths and feel ready to help someone else down their path to awesome, there are three simple ways to start.

## Ask a question.

The greatest way to ensure you fail at something new is to attempt to be an expert at it on day one. While we see the absurdity of that approach in physical activities like running—no one wakes up one day having never run and completes a marathon that afternoon—in other areas, we often believe we must go zero to 100 mph in a matter of seconds.

That's what happens with guiding. We've never guided someone else before, and yet we feel the need to one day. We look up the definition of *mentoring* and then think to ourselves, *I just need to find someone who needs my advice and encouragement. We'll have coffee every morning for the next sixty years, form the kind of friendship that makes you want to jump on a grenade for each other, and then we'll be buried next to each other in the cemetery. He ain't heavy; he's my brother!*

The weight of that task feels overwhelming, as it should, so we give up before we even begin.

Not you though. Not me either. We're not going to go into Guiding like that. All we're going to do is ask one person one question.

Someone once told me that the secret to being humble is remembering that it's not all about you. "It's" meaning the world, the day, the conversation at the copier machine at work, the traffic jam you're stuck in, etc.

My friend said that in order to really believe it's not all about you, you have to believe that everyone is more interesting than you. The person who cleans your room at a hotel, the guy next to you in traffic, the businessman who sits next to you on a plane. Everyone.

I thought this was an impossible feat and, honestly, kind of dumb advice. It sounded like the kind of thing people who are secretly arrogant say when they're trying to pretend they're humble. *Everyone* is more interesting than you? Come on. I've met some boring people; so have you. How in the world do you see everyone as more interesting than you?

It just seemed silly, even when I heard brilliant minds like Jim Collins talk about this very issue. Once, while seeking wisdom about how to be a better teacher, Jim Collins was told by Stanford professor Jim Gardner, "It occurs to me, Jim, that you spend too much time trying to be interesting. Why don't you invest more time being interested?"[2]

I still didn't get it, though.

Then, one night on a plane ride from Denver, it suddenly made sense.

How so? Well, I've always got access to me. I'm with me all the time. I can't get away from me. I'm with me 24/7. But the lady on the plane who teaches special-needs college students, who is flying home to join her twin sister and the rest of her family to welcome her brother home from Iraq where he's been a fighter pilot? I'll probably never see her again.

She's got a really interesting story. And I'll never, ever get to hear it again unless I ask her a question and then listen to what she's all about.

Most of the people you bump into on an average day are only going to be there for a second or a minute. And then they're gone, swept back into the rest of the day. And you've only got a moment to hear their stories, a second to pause your busy life long enough to hear about somebody else's and maybe even contribute to it with a bit of guiding. Your access is incredibly limited. And they are more interesting than you. I promise.

That covers intersections with strangers, but what about the people we see all the time? Coworkers, friends, family members. Why are they so interesting?

Because you already know your stories. You've heard them a dozen times. What could they possibly tell you? Well, the coworker who is so sarcastic he's practically surly—do you know that guy? Is he at your office too? He was at mine. He's going to cry at lunch when you ask him how he's doing, because it turns out he's walking away from the wreckage of a second divorce, and he's exhausted carrying his story alone. It's really heavy. And he'd gladly share it with you if you weren't so focused on thinking it's all about you.

It's not.

If you'll ask people a question, more often than not they'll tell you a story that will blow you away or make you laugh or cry or a million other things. More often than not, whether it's a conversation on a plane with a stranger you'll never see again or a coworker you've seen for years, that question you ask will begin a conversation. And guiding always starts with a conversation.

Want to guide? Ask one person one question.

## Tie guiding to something you already care about.

For months, my friend Stephen and I tried to get breakfast regularly. We're both in a similar spot in life right now and could use some mutual guidance. For months we weren't able to.

Something always came up. Our weeks got too full. It was hard to ever get on a regular schedule, until we tied that moment of guidance to something unexpected—the gym.

Instead of going to breakfast, we decided to work out together. We decided that two to three times a week, we'd meet at the Y at 6:15 a.m. We'd spend forty-five minutes talking, exercising, and hanging out. That may sound like a small change, but the success rate of it has been tremendous.

We're still the same people with the same busy weeks, but tying guiding to the gym changed everything. Because we both know we need to work out regularly. We didn't need to eat pancakes regularly. We both were already interested in exercise. And going to the gym two to three times a week is something you can do without getting weird. Eating at Cracker Barrel three times a week with the same person is weird. How much old-timey maple syrup does one person need?

I'm not the only one who does this. My wife goes on ten-mile power walks with her friend Emily a few times a week (I didn't think this qualified as exercise until I tried it and nearly died). Other people will take an art class together or volunteer at an animal shelter together. If you're going to be successful at guiding, don't be afraid to tie it to something else that gives you momentum.

While guiding is a natural consequence of being awesome, let's not kid ourselves that every morning for the rest of your life you'll wake up with a spring in your step and a song in your heart about helping others. Some mornings it's my desire for my pants to not be so tight that the top button pops off and kills somebody. That gets me to the gym, not the desire to guide someone. But once I'm at the gym, I'm always glad Stephen and I both make the effort to help each other along the road to awesome.

## Pick your spots carefully.

In the land of Editing, we honed our passions down with laser-like focus. Guiding requires the same level of intentionality, unless you want to feel like a jerk for a few years.

That was my initial experience with helping others. After my first book came out, people online started to ask me questions about how to write a book. That's fun, but I approached guiding too casually.

I wasn't deliberate about the places I provided guidance. I tried to help people everywhere and ended up not succeeding anywhere.

I couldn't respond to all the questions on Twitter, and that made me feel like a jerk.

I couldn't respond to all the questions on my blog, and that made me feel like a jerk.

I couldn't respond to all the emails I got, and that made me feel like a jerk.

Turns out, the best way to always miss your target is to make sure you never establish one.

You will be swamped with opportunities to guide other people. Maybe not at first. It took months and months for a stranger to ask me to grab coffee so he could "pick my brain." But it will happen, and I want you to be ready with a few boundaries so you can do the greatest good possible.

I made my boundaries simple.

I don't give long, detailed advice on Twitter, because it's not a long, detailed medium. When someone sends me a tweet that says, "Can you please tell me how to write a book?" it's impossible to successfully fulfill that request via a 140-character reply. Trying, and then feeling bad about the inevitable failure, is a waste of time and energy.

I don't go to breakfast every day, or lunch or coffee. I once heard a pastor say, "I'd love to go to coffee with every one of you, but then I'd never have time to do all the things that make you want to have coffee with me in the first place. Like studying, reading, researching, and helping the people I've committed to." Instead, I have a lunch window open every Friday for strangers who ask for guidance. That's a potential lunch with fifty-two new people a year. Instead of it floating around on the calendar and tangling me up with scheduling headaches, I know exactly when I'm available.

I also disappoint the right people. I learned this trick by signing up for something called the "Warrior Dash." It's a 5K obstacle course that involves mud, fire, water, and Viking helmets. I signed up for it months before the race date, but twenty-four hours before the event, I decided not to go.

Why? Because it's important to disappoint the right people in my life.

For years, I thought if I lived a perfect life, I could make everyone happy and never disappoint anyone. I know that's a foolish thought, but people-pleasers like me are constantly intoxicated with expectations like that.

But the day before the race, I realized something: I was going to be out of town for the next three weekends. I speak at the Dave Ramsey live events, and we were headed out to visit three different cities.

I had a choice to make. I could either disappoint my kids—who need guiding—and tell them, "Hey, on the Saturday before I'm gone for three Saturdays in a row, I'm going to spend five hours running in a race instead of hanging out with you." Or, I could disappoint my friends and tell them, "I've got to bail on the Warrior Dash."

I decided to disappoint my friends.

Instead of doing the race, I spent the entire Saturday with my wife and kids at a botanical garden. It was an amazing day, and I felt instantly that I had made the right decision.

As you guide, you're going to disappoint people who want your time or your input or your attendance. And often you won't be able to give it to them. But it's okay to disappoint people, as long as you make sure you're disappointing (and guiding) the right people.

The biggest lesson for me was to not say yes to things I am ultimately going to say no to. When my friends asked me to run in the race, I should have looked at my calendar, seen the travel I had scheduled, and said no. But I didn't want to disappoint them. My initial yes only amplified the disappointment of me eventually saying no twenty-four hours before the race.

Don't tell polite lies, like "Let's grab coffee sometime," when you have no intention of doing that. Pick your guiding spots carefully, and then stick to them.

## FAST RUNNERS

You got your start in guiding with a single question. You then tied guiding to something you're already interested in, and you picked your spots carefully. Now, how do you know you're guiding? How do you know you're really helping others? The other lands tend to have discernible signs. What about guiding?

I think the best way to know if you're really helping people is to observe the pace of everyone else who is running with you.

In the 2012 Summer Olympics, Kenyan David Rudisha set the world record in the 800-meter race. On the surface, that is not so amazing. Lots of records were set during the games, and lots of people got gold medals. Usain Bolt got considerably more press than Rudisha. But in many ways, Rudisha's race was far more amazing not because of what he accomplished with his running, but because of what his running inspired in every other runner in the race. Seven of the eight runners set their personal bests during the race. The last-place runner was the fastest last place in the history of the event.[3]

David Symmonds, the American, came in fifth, which isn't great until you look at the history books. Symmonds's fifth-place time would have won him a gold medal in 2008. And 2004. And 2000. In fact, Symmonds's fifth-place finish would have been good enough for a gold in every Olympics, except one, since 1896.[4]

How were so many athletes able to achieve so much in one race?

Someone set the pace a little ahead of them. Or as the *Guardian* reported, "Rudisha pulled the field around behind him, like a speedboat leading seven water-skiers."[5]

The other runners couldn't help but raise their game that night. Rudisha's pursuit of awesome was infectious.

You may not feel qualified to guide. But please know that in the land of Guiding you have the chance to do something even more important.

You have the chance to change the world.

You never get to change the world before you change your life. Now that you've walked through four lands and are standing in the fifth and final land, you've changed your life quite significantly. Now it's time to change the world.

People are mistaken when they think chasing your dream is a selfish thing to do. As if perhaps being average is an act of humility. As if perhaps wasting the talents you were given is proof that you're a considerate individual.

It's not.

"If you were meant to cure cancer or write a symphony or crack cold fusion and you don't," asserts Steven Pressfield, "you not only hurt yourself, even destroy yourself; you hurt your children. You hurt me. You hurt the planet. Creative work is not a selfish act or a bid for attention on the part of the actor. It's a gift to the world and every being in it. Don't cheat us of your contribution. Give us what you've got."[6]

## HERE'S WHAT'S NEXT FOR YOU

1. Find someone to guide.
2. Take another part of your life back to the start, and journey down the road to awesome again.

That's it.

Those are the only things we ultimately do in the land of Guiding.

We just talked about the first step. That one is pretty easy. If anything, the hardest part will be deciding which people to guide. People who notice you're not average tend to want to take you out to coffee and ask, "What's different about you?"

The second is actually an invitation to the fountain of youth. Turns out it's not in Florida; it's on the road to awesome in whichever state or country you live.

The only way to stay young is to keep learning. That's not last-chapter hyperbole—that's science. In the book *Ten Steps Ahead*, Erik Calonius wrote, "Even though the number of neurons in the human brain decreases as we age (as has been said time and again), the number of synaptic connections can grow as long as we live. If we keep using our noodle, in other words, we can make our brain better every day."

Neuroscientists Steven Quartz and Terrance Sejnowski report, "Being born some way doesn't amount to forever remaining that way. . . . Your experiences with the world alter your brain's structure, chemistry, and genetic expression, often profoundly throughout your life."

And most encouraging—given that the first land on the road to awesome is Learning—is what New York University neurologist Joseph LeDoux has to say on the matter: "Learning allows us to transcend our genes."[7]

In other words, the land of Learning can keep you younger than your genes say you are.

Science aside, it's easy to look at the end of someone's life and see how important it is to keeping walking down the road to awesome.

I think of my friend Brent's grandfather. He was a decorated World War II vet who went on to be an All-American college football player who was elected to the College Football Hall of Fame. He then had an incredibly successful and widely respected medical practice in San Diego for forty-four years. After he was forced to give up his practice because he was just "getting too old" at 77, he immediately started to decline. Within two years, he was dead. When I asked Brent about it, he said simply, "I think he died because he couldn't find the next thing to start."

That's why my grandmother takes Tai Chi. She may be 85 in birth years, but she's 22 in Tai Chi years. She's brand-new on that particular road to awesome. She knows that ultimately the road is a circle, not a straight line. Will she master Tai Chi? Will she one day guide in it? I don't know, but I didn't know she'd spend our Christmas phone call asking me about a reader from my blog who comments a lot either. His name is Michael, and she was a little worried about him. Turns out she's 22 in blogging too.

I'm not sure what you need to take back down the road to awesome, but I do know it works with more than just your career or passion. Awesome marriages go through the same five lands. No awesome marriage is ever accidental. Awesome companies go through the same five lands too. Steve Jobs was a genius at editing, reducing the entire Apple product offering to just four brilliant lines. Awesome families go through the same five lands. Average families are the norm; awesome families follow a map.

I hope you punched fear in the face. I hope you escaped average. I hope you figured out what your diamonds are and started doing work that matters. I hope you realized the door to purpose has been unlocked this whole time.

And when you survey your life and find something else that could be more awesome, I hope you'll do what I'm going to do once I finish writing this sentence.

Start again.

# WHAT NOW?

# ACTION ALWAYS BEATS INTENTION

**ANYONE CAN DREAM.** It's the doing that is such a hassle. Where do you start? What do you do next? What will keep you from heading right back to the road to average?

This.

This will.

In these pages are practical, tactical steps you can take. Some are simple, like writing down a single idea on a Post-it note; others are more detailed, like tracking your time for seventy-two hours. But each one is designed to jump-start your travel down the road to awesome. This is where inspiration meets instruction, hope meets hard work, dreaming meets doing.

Let's go.

## PUNCH FEAR IN THE FACE

1. Buy a journal. You'll keep walking in circles unless you document your experience.

2. Answer the question, "What do my voices of fear and doubt tell me?" Every time you bump into one, write it down.

3. Mock each fear you write down. If you're afraid you'll lose your job and never be able to find a new one if you launch a new project at work, write that out. Exaggerate that fear in the craziest ways possible so you can see how silly it is. "If the project fails, I'll get fired and blacklisted from that entire industry. All companies, in every city, in every country will not hire me. I will be forever unemployed and have to grow a really crazy beard and collect cats."

4. Once you're done laughing at your fears, make them face the truth. Next to each one, write what is true (e.g., "Everyone will laugh at me if I try this new dream." Truth = "My friends won't laugh. My sister won't laugh. I just proved that 'everyone' was a lie."). (See pages 70–71 for more examples of how I do this.)

5. Look for patterns in your voices. Fear always likes to pretend it's brand-new each time. It's not. Chances are you'll be able to identify four or five primary fears at the root of every voice.

6. Fear masquerades as new because it wants you to waste energy looking for a new way to fight it. Now that we know we've seen it before, we can look for a successful tool we've used in the past to combat it. What's something that has worked for you before that could work for you today?

7. Identify a "mirror friend," someone who will reflect the truth of your experience back to you. This is a friend who will listen and then help you see the situation you're in for what it really is.

8. Share the voices of fear and doubt you run into with your mirror friend or someone else you trust.

9. Think you're the only one who hears a certain voice of fear? Visit nomorevoices.com and see that you're not alone. Find your voice and share it with a community of people who are on the road to awesome just like you.

10. Fear is schizophrenic—it always tries to argue both sides of the coin. It will tell you that you can't chase your dream or that if you do, it must be perfect. Knock its legs out by writing down the opposite things it is saying to you right now (e.g., "It's too late to chase your dream" and "You should chase your dream later").

## ESCAPE AVERAGE

1. If we're going to escape average, we need to know where we feel like average has crept into our lives. Do an "average audit." Survey the seven key areas of your life: physical, spiritual, financial, family, social, intellectual, and career. Write down which ones feel average. (We'll need this list when we get down to step 6 in this section.)

2. Be brutally realistic about your present circumstances. List out your current debts (e.g., student loans, mortgage, credit card, etc.). List out your current roles (e.g., father, husband, coach, etc.). List out your current assets that may contribute to your dream (e.g., college degree, blog, network of friends, expertise in field, etc.). The goal of this is to paint the clearest, most honest picture of where you are right now. (See pages 35–43 for more background on this principle.)

3. Be wildly unrealistic about your future circumstances. We're going to take dozens of steps toward our dream in the weeks to come, but right now, just free write every crazy thing you'd like to do (e.g., you've never played guitar before, but someday you want to play the Ryman Auditorium in Nashville, Tennessee). Everything you wrote down during step 2 doesn't exist.

4. Recognize that there will ALWAYS be tension in your life between steps 2 and 3. Do regular temperature checks to

and walk away encouraged. If they say, "Yes, of course! I predicted this years ago!" keep looking for someone honest.

9.  Standing on the shoulders of a giant is one of the ways you can accelerate your journey down the road to awesome. Who in your life right now may be a giant? Someone who has already traveled the same path you're on and could share some advice with you?

10. Write one giant in your life a thank-you note today. Nothing kills the toxin of ego like gratefulness, and we've all been helped by at least one person in our lives.

11. Before we jump into the land of Learning, make sure your feet are on the ground. Have you climbed the rungs of an entitlement ladder anywhere in your life? If you asked friends if you were on an entitlement ladder, what would they say?

## THE LAND OF LEARNING

1.  Do a seventy-two-hour audit, writing down the thirty-minute chunks of time you spend over a three-day period (two work days and one weekend day). Example: Monday, thirty-minute commute, eight hours of work, one hour lunch break, etc. (If you have the patience to do a weeklong audit, that's even better.)

make sure you have not pendulum swung too far in ther direction.

5. One of the first things that happens when we escape ave age is that we face the "great wall of purpose." Which of tl five purpose lies from pages 47–49 do you struggle wi the most? (1. Everyone but you knows exactly what his i 2. You'll only have one; 3. You should have it figured ol by the time you're 22 years old; 4. It changes everythin instantly; 5. You have to know the finish lines before yol cross the starting line.)

6. Every big finish began with a small start. Looking at the results of your "average audit," what's an area where you want to make a small start? We tend to see the whole mountain first, not the first step. Write down a list of first steps you could take (e.g., lose one pound, update one section of your resume, ask one person on a date, etc.).

7. Write "Some beats none" on a Post-it note and place it ol your alarm clock, computer, or fridge. When fear tells yo that if you don't have time to run five miles today, the you shouldn't bother running two, remind it that "son beats none."

8. Ask one successful person in your life if at the start their journey they knew exactly where they'd be stan ing today. If they say, "No, of course not," hug the

2. Review the result of your audit and find your "5 a.m.," which is thirty minutes you can rescue to work on your dream each week.

3. Immediately realize there are more than thirty minutes available. Rescue as much time as you want.

4. Create a clear picture of why you're getting up early or staying up late to work on your dream. For example, I hate getting up early. But I tend to go to bed earlier if I remember that it means I get to write more in the morning, which I love doing. Be hyper-clear about the reward that is behind the work. Write in your journal, "I'm being selfish at 5 a.m. because _____."

5. Write a list of all the things you won't get done now that you're focusing more on things that matter (e.g., "It will take me forty-eight hours to respond to emails instead of twenty-four hours because I'm going to work on my business plan instead of obsessively checking email."). Don't feel ashamed or guilty about what balls you may drop. Drop them on purpose.

6. Crash your plane. Answer the question, "If I died today, what would I regret not being able to do?" Write down one to five answers. If you have more, that's fine; you may just need to spend more time in Editing (page 86).

7. Take your list from step 6 and honestly ask yourself, "Are those the things I'm spending time doing right now?" If the

answer is yes, awesome. If the answer is no, ask yourself, "Why not?" What's keeping you from doing those things?

8. Answer the question, "What can't I stop doing?" (pages 91–92)

9. Be a student of you. Think back to the most successful project, idea, diet, or goal you ever completed. What did you learn about the way you work best in that situation that can be applied to this one? Example: I was able to lose weight when I had a team of people cheering me on. If I'm going to work on being awesome at _____, I need to put together a team of supporters in order to succeed (page 92).

10. Take what you learn from step 9 and apply it to every tactic I share going forward. If you work best with low details, go lower than I suggest. If you work best with high details, go more detailed in the actions I suggest. Customize this section of the book to your strengths.

11. Identify one small, nonfatal experiment you can do this week with your dream (page 100). Starting a blog is an example of a good one. Me starting an ad agency with a near stranger is a bad example because it proved to be fatal to our friendship.

12. Give yourself copious amounts of grace for the moments you will inevitably stumble back onto the road to average without realizing it. Perfection will tell you nobody else does that. That's a lie. Perfect isn't the goal or even

possible. Awesome is, and even awesome makes mistakes along the way.

## THE LAND OF EDITING

1. Ask this question first: "What gives me the most joy?" Don't ask, "What am I good at right now?" or "What will make me the most money?" or "What will cause the least inconvenience in my life?"

2. What dream for you would actually be a park bench? What dream is your version of Frisbee golf (pages 110–11)? For instance, I wrote technical copy for companies for years, but that was a park bench for me. It was good work, and I got paid well, but it wasn't something that fit what I felt called to do.

3. Finish this sentence: "This would never work, but I've always wanted to _____."

4. Find an anti-mentor—someone you never want to end up like. Write down what it is about their life that you fear will become true of yours. With that answer, what are some obvious steps you can take to ensure that doesn't happen? (Side note: Never tell someone they are your anti-mentor. For some crazy reason, people don't like that.)

5. Write a list of your diamonds (e.g., family, friendships, work, etc.) (pages 121–22).

6. Now write a list of your rocks (e.g., having zero emails in my inbox, taking care of my yard, keeping up with the Joneses, etc.).

7. Write down that same list, only this time use the time audit you did in the land of Learning as your guide. Are there any big discrepancies between what you think your diamonds are and what your calendar really says they are? If so, what do you want to do about them?

8. Have you ever chased someone else's diamonds? Have you ever chased someone else's dream because you were afraid to chase your own? Make sure the dream you're editing is your own and not your mom's, your dad's, or a teacher's you had who said, "You'd be good at _____."

9. Go into the observatory tower and write a "wild success paragraph" for each diamond you identified in steps 5 and 7. If you were wildly successful with each idea, which one would generate the most joy in your life (and subsequently other people's lives)?

10. Answer the "mountain climber questions." What's something you'd still do even if no one ever clapped? What's something you'd still do if you never made a dollar? What's something you'd still do if you never earned a second in the spotlight (pages 131–33)?

11. Create your own seesaw. If you had to pick two passions and put them on either side of a seesaw, which one would you want to win (pages 130–31)?

12. Build a "later list" to store all the good ideas you might explore the next time you edit your life.

13. Write a paragraph describing who your "secret self" really is (pages 133–34).

## THE LAND OF MASTERING

1. Admit you feel like the only one who read this book and wasn't able to find just one thing they want to master. Realize that's not true and proceed with the tactics anyway.

2. Figure out if there's a way to volunteer somewhere in order to get better at what you're passionate about. If the answer is yes, decide if you have the time to do that.

3. Decide if there is a part-time job you could take to move you down the road to awesome. Don't be so quick to dismiss this one if your goal isn't career-related. If your goal is to lose weight and there's a part-time job that would force you to be physically active, it may be a good fit.

4. Survey your life and decide if there's ever been something you experienced that made you think, *I could do that*

*better.* Was that the start of a dream that needs to be explored, like the taxi driver on pages 141–42, or just a fleeting observation?

5. Find and attend one event centered around whatever it is you're trying to master.

6. Set a "rep" goal for the month. Write down every rep you do and what you learned from the experience (page 146).

7. Create a list of people who are doing what you'd like to do. Research one to three things from each of these people that you can incorporate into your own road to awesome.

8. Scribble down "Who said it?" and "Why did they say it?" on a Post-it note. Stick that note to your computer for the next time someone criticizes your dream.

9. Beat critic's math by reversing the numbers. Take the negative feedback you received and divide it by all the positive feedback. For example, three Amazon one-star reviews of my last book divided by the total number of books I sold means 0.004 percent of people hated it. If my daughter got a 99.996 on a test, I wouldn't worry about that 0.004 percent she missed. Find your real number and write it down. Then laugh at how silly it is to let 0.004 percent of people control your day.

10. Start a preemptive thank-you list. By the time you hit Harvesting, you may think you accomplished all of this on

your own. You didn't. Create a list of the people you need to thank when you are successful.

11. Start looking for a fellow traveler, someone who is hustling on their own dream. Mirror friends are critical, but a fellow traveler will have trench wisdom and advice that a mirror friend might not have.

12. Sacrifice is an accelerant. Create a list of things you are willing to sacrifice in the pursuit of awesome. Later, when you're mad that you didn't get to go somewhere or do something because you were focused on the long-term win, review this list and remember why.

13. Create a full box of ammo for why you won't give up before you get to awesome. Some days, "working so my kids have a brighter future" will be enough. Other days, "friends who hold me accountable" will be enough. In the moments when it gets hard to keep going, you'll be glad you have 101 reasons to not quit.

14. Identify a little bit of Central Park in your life (page 157).

15. Write down three of your expectations for the road ahead. For example, "I expect to have a new job in the next six months at a company in Austin, Texas." Detail them as specifically as possible to make sure you're not harboring any "secret" expectations (pages 158–61).

## THE LAND OF HARVESTING

1. No one gives up when they can see the finish line. If your harvest feels far away, create a series of small finish lines so that each day or week can have a bit of harvest hidden in it. Example: Writing a book takes forever, so I made chapter finish lines and sometimes even daily word count finish lines to keep me going.

2. Ask your mirror friend or fellow travelers if they feel like you've taken any exits or climbed any entitlement ladders along the road to awesome (pages 170–73).

3. Don't be a jerk. Repeat as necessary.

4. That last one was easy, right? Probably took you ten seconds. To take it even further, ask someone who loves you enough to tell you something you may not like to hear, "Am I being a jerk these days?"

5. Make a list of the "action payments" you're paying toward your dream. If the list is small, don't complain when the harvest is too. If that's not okay with you, make more payments (pages 174–75).

6. Build a brag table (pages 184–85).

7. If the harvest doesn't feel as big as you wish it were, give yourself the "10,000 hours test," using Ericsson's principle

of how long expertise takes. Add up all the hours you've worked on your dream. If it's less than 10,000, don't worry about the size of your harvest. You've got some more mastering to do. If it's greater than 10,000 and the harvest is still small, be patient. Weeds grow quickly; the best crops take longer.

8. Make a list of the things that got you to Harvesting that you no longer need to do and those that you must continue. Example: To grow my blog community, I initially used to comment on dozens of blogs. As it grew and I had my own traffic, I had to stop commenting on other blogs so much and instead focus on writing my blog more.

9. Check to make sure "self-sabotage" has not reared its ugly head. Are there any situations right now where you're drilling holes in your own ship? If the answer is yes, call it what it is—"fear of success"—and punch it in the face.

10. Review your diamond and rock list to make sure any unwanted changes have not happened to your priorities along the way.

## THE LAND OF GUIDING

1. Make sure the stuff you acquired in the land of Harvesting (money, accolades, fame, success, etc.) are merely

consequences of being awesome, not your reason to be. Great things mutate into great exits if we're not careful.

2. When is the last time you failed? Have you been carrying it around too long? Or are you coasting based on a success you experienced? If so, avoid both exits back to average by launching another small experiment for your dream (pages 209–10).

3. Using the "student of you" technique, write down three of the best ways you could guide someone else. Example: I'm great at one-on-one interactions; I'm best at speaking to groups of ten or less, etc.

4. Write a list of three people you could guide in your life right now.

5. List three successes you could share with someone.

6. List three failures you could share with someone.

7. Pick one day a week that you will set aside time to deliberately guide someone else. Example: Every Friday morning you go out to breakfast with someone who needs some advice or encouragement. It won't happen unless you're intentional.

8. Create a list of people you're okay with disappointing as you spend time being deliberate with how you guide (pages 212–14).

9.  Identify a new part of your life to take back down the road to awesome. Review the "later list" from the land of Editing, if you created one.

10. Review the journal you've been keeping. Or blog or whatever form of record worked best for how you tracked progress. If you're going to march down the road again, it helps to know where the dragons and potholes are so you can avoid them on the second trip.

11. Start again.

# APPENDIX A

# 10 WAYS TO ACCELERATE AWESOME WITH SOCIAL MEDIA

**I WISH I COULD PUT A SIGN IN MY YARD** that says, "I know about Google." That way, whoever keeps delivering forty-two-pound yellow pages to my house could skip our driveway. Every time we get one it goes right to the recycling bin because by the time it's printed, it's out of date. Books about social media usually suffer from the same problem. The whole industry is moving so quickly right now that by the time the ink dries on your sentence telling people to "build a presence on MySpace," Facebook has murdered it. (One notable exception to this problem is Michael Hyatt's book *Platform*.)

So rather than tips about specific technologies that will be out-of-date tomorrow, here are the ten principles I used to build my

tribe and accelerate my awesome. These are the principles that dominated the first decade of social media and will continue to play a critical role in the next 100 years.

## 1. Understand why you're using social media in the first place.

In the great book *Start with Why*, Simon Sinek encourages readers to ask why before they start any new endeavor. That logic certainly holds true with social media. Most businesses and individuals jump online, sign up for thirty-two different platforms, and never stop to ask that question. "Why am I using social media?" Is it a fun way to keep up with relatives? Are you trying to connect with potential customers? Are you trying to service existing customers? Are you trying to build a platform that will make your next job interview even easier? The answers to that question are endless, but the one that matters most for you is yours. What's your goal with social media? Mine is to help jumpstart people who feel stuck. "Jumpstart" means I'm great at the initial creative moment that helps someone get unstuck but not great at the twenty-year follow-up plan. So I tend to stick to online tools that offer short bursts of information. Like Twitter. On the flip side, I failed at a blog concept I came up with called "#FinishYear" because writing about the same exact subject for an entire year isn't what I'm great at. Get your social media goal roughly shaped, and then you can really start to apply the rest of the principles.

## 2. Pick your places.

The most overwhelming part of social media is that by the time you finish reading this sentence some new technology will be

popular. You'll put this book down, and your hipster friend will say, "You're not on double upside-down orange 2.9? You still use Facebook? Ugh, no one uses that." We all have "profile exhaustion," the sense of tiredness we feel when someone sends us an invitation to yet another social media platform we should have a presence on. Let's put that concern to bed right now—you don't have to be everywhere at once online. You just have to pick your places. Depending on your goals, pick one to three places you want to be involved. If you're a business, go where your customers already are. If you're an individual, go where your passion is. Don't buy the "all or nothing" myth of social media. Pick your places carefully. (My places are Twitter, my blog jonacuff.com, and Pinterest. I do next to nothing right now on Facebook.)

### 3. Play to your strengths.

Make social media play to your strengths, not the other way around. For instance, I am a horrible photographer. I will never make it onto the popular page of Instagram with the quality of my photography. I'm a writer. That's my strength. So rather than waste time trying to become an amazing photographer, I do something completely different. I write simple, spreadable thoughts on Post-it notes. Then I take a photo of that note and post it on Instagram. Those photos get more "likes" than any other photos I do. Why? Because I'm a writer who found a way to "write" on a photo-based platform. Don't think you have to develop some completely different talent to dominate social media. Make the platform obey the strength you already have.

## 4. Focus on your content strategy before your promotion strategy.

Imagine you owned a store. You were having a grand opening. You spent hours and hours promoting your big day. You spent thousands of dollars inviting people to the ribbon cutting, doing everything you could to drive traffic to your location. The day arrived, the parking lot was slammed full of people, it was a wild success . . . and then you opened the doors. And all the shelves were empty. In the excitement of promoting your store, you forgot to stock it. You've got an immaculate layout. The design is unbelievable . . . but it doesn't matter. People were expecting products. And as soon as they took a look behind the curtain, so to speak, and realized the store was empty, they left and never came back.

That's what content is in the world of social media. Content = products.

Even if you never want to sell a single thing via social media, if you want to build a community, you have to have a foundation to build it on. And that foundation is the content.

If you start with the promotion, the building will be well known and well ignored. If you start with the design, the building will be beautiful and empty. If you start with the community, the building will be temporarily crowded but eventually abandoned.

Content is king. Content is currency.

Content is critical. In the old-school, "Who? What? When? Where? Why?" model of journalism, content is the "What?" What blogs will you write? What videos will you share? What will you create?

## 5. Be honest.

One of the challenges with social media is that it's hard to stand out. I Googled the phrase "mom blog," and there were 341 million results. Every month, millions of people join Facebook and Twitter. YouTube has 92 billion page views per month. How do you possibly stand out in the middle of that clutter?

The answer most commonly given is "talent."

You have to have the most talent or the best talent or the greatest talent. And thirty years ago, maybe that was true. But in the last twenty years, honesty has become as important as talent. Why?

Well, thanks to the Internet and globalization, we now have more access to more talent than we've ever had in the history of mankind. Think about it. Do you know where that band you found online was playing their music twenty years ago? In their garage—you didn't know they existed. Twenty years ago, that director who makes funny clips for Youtube or Funny or Die, you know where he was showing his movies? In his living room. You didn't have access to his work. Do you know where your favorite blog writer was writing her thoughts twenty years ago? In her diary. On her nightstand. She was still writing amazing stuff, but you couldn't read it.

In the last twenty years, we've all gained more access to more talent than we can possibly fathom. (Granted, there's a lot of nonsense too.) But what's happened is that the talent pool is really full right now. It's crowded. There's not a whole lot of room to splash around in that one. The honesty pool?

That's a completely different story. You can do the backstroke in that one. You've got all the room in the world. No one would say that in the last twenty years we've become more honest as a culture. (Shows like *TMZ* have exposed more dirty laundry, but being caught is not the same thing as being honest.)

So if you want to stand out online, if you really want to make a splash with social media, be honest.

This isn't new information. The best marketers in the world already know this and are racing to honesty as fast as they can. Take Nike, for instance.

In the '90s, companies like Nike and Gatorade used to tell you to "be like Mike." The advertising was over-the-top, practically promising that if you bought the Air Jordan, you'd probably be able to dunk the next day. And we believed it. We believed it to such a strong degree that kids started shooting each other for the sneakers.

Do you know what the headline for a recent Nike campaign was? "This shoe works if you do."

Wait, what? Where's the bravado? Where's the promise? Where's the hype? That's a 180-degree change from the ads they used to run. But they know that this generation has the sharpest marketing radar ever. They want honesty. That's what's going to stand out, and Nike knows that.

Be honest online. That was the biggest reason my first blog grew. I talked honestly about some of the ridiculous things we did in the name of faith, and people hadn't seen much of that online before.

Social media is either a megaphone or a mask. It will amplify what you're all about or hide what you're all about. Be honest and amplify.

## 6. Don't think of social media as a silver bullet.

When the readers of my blog built those two kindergartens in Vietnam, the *Atlanta Journal-Constitution* wrote an article about the first kindergarten. The headline was "Blogger raises $30,000 in 18 hours." Technically, that headline was true, but it should have read, "Blogger raises $30,000 in 18 months."

That's how long it really took to raise the money. For eighteen months, I consistently wrote *Stuff Christians Like*. I poured a million words of the best ideas I could think of into the conversation with readers. Day after day, post after post, with consistency, I jumped into the discussion happening on *Stuff Christians Like*.

I didn't show up one day out of the blue and say, "Hi, my name is Jon. You've never heard of me. Give me money for a kindergarten," but sometimes we think that's how social media works. We watch certain ideas go viral and think our business, cause, or blog should go viral too. We want social media to be a silver bullet. Here's the truth:

Social media isn't a silver bullet. It's a million free bullets.

If you try something for a month and give up, you won't change the world. If you write a blog for ninety days and quit, you won't change the world. If you fool around with Twitter for a week and then stop, you won't change the world.

It takes time. It takes grind. And it takes a commitment to consistency.

## 7. Don't reinvent the wheel.

When we discussed our plans to build a microsite for this book, do you know what the first question we asked was?

"How did Michael Hyatt design his microsite?" Why did we ask that? Because he's a genius, and you should never reinvent the wheel in social media. We knew that he and other authors had very deliberately crafted their microsites. We could study theirs, add our own unique aspects, and skip weeks of needless guessing. If you've got the answer to the first question—why you're using social media—and you understand what your content is, start researching. Find other social media giants in your sphere who are already doing brilliant work, and then build on it.

## 8. Once you know what you're all about, make sure others do too.

A few months ago I had dinner with a friend of mine. He's a social media consultant. He gets paid thousands and thousands of dollars to help companies with their social media strategies. During the middle of the meal, he leaned forward and confessed something quietly, "I know I'm supposed to be using Google Plus, but I just don't know what I'm supposed to be doing."

And as silly as that may sound, I feel the same way.

I'm pretty sure it's awesome. I mean, it's Google, after all! Who doesn't love Google? But whenever I check in or log in or whatever verb you use when interacting with Plus, I don't really know what I'm supposed to do.

I'm positive there must be some stream of conversation going on somewhere within the platform. There must be some reason it's awesome, but I can't find it. So, after a few minutes of poking around, I return to the platforms I do know how to use, Twitter and Pinterest.

And it turns out, so do a lot of other people. The *Wall Street Journal* reported, "visitors using personal computers spent an average of about three minutes a month on Google Plus between September and January, versus six to seven hours on Facebook each month over the same period, according to comScore, which didn't have data on mobile usage."[1]

Will Google Plus bounce back? Maybe. That team is brilliant, but if they bounce back by the time this book comes out, it will be because they fixed one thing: clarity.

Clarity is the way you carve out some space in the cluttered social media world. It's how you tell readers and followers and fans and customers, "This is what I'm all about." It's your idea stripped down to its bare essentials, so that the most distracted generation in the history of mankind can instantly understand where you fit in the social media landscape.

This one takes time. No blog ends up a year later being exactly the way you planned it. No social media campaign does exactly what you expected it would. The only way you develop your voice is by using your voice. And often you have to use that voice for six months to a year until you've got clarity.

What does this look like for an individual like you?

Allow me to share the first thirty words you see at the top of the blog *Pocket-Sized Stories*: "When you teach kindergarten, the things that you bring home in your pockets every day tell that day's story. Every day, I'll empty my pockets and tell my story."[2]

That is perfect. Who is writing this blog? A kindergarten teacher.

What is it about? The things he has in his pockets at the end of the day.

Why is that interesting? Because those things tell a story.

In less than thirty words, the author of the blog gives an incredibly compelling reason to read his blog.

Is that important today?

Yes. And it will be even more important tomorrow because, every day, 100,000 new blogs are started. Clarity is a great way to differentiate yourself from the masses. Although it's harder to explain your blog when it has multiple topics (leadership, parenting, writing, etc.), it still needs to be done.

Can you summarize your approach to social media in thirty words or less?

## 9. Recognize the ridiculous power of context.

Context changes everything, and I learned that in a maternity ward in Boston almost nine years ago.

My wife had given birth to our first daughter, L.E., in Brigham and Women's, a hospital right near Fenway Park. As I was returning to the room with ice chips (the only real value I was able to provide in those first twenty-four hours), I noticed something out the window. I walked over to the edge of the waiting room and couldn't believe what I saw.

Eight stories down from where I was standing was a billboard for a Toyota minivan. What surprised me about it was how it was positioned. You couldn't see it from the street. If you were driving through Boston, you couldn't read the billboard or really even tell what it was for. The angle from the street was horrible, but some advertising genius didn't care about the street. They cared about the waiting room I was in right that second.

The billboard was tilted perfectly to grab my attention. The billboard was aimed right at that window, a window where new dads and new moms and new grandparents were sitting. People who suddenly had a deep need for a minivan. People who had entered a new season of life and were suddenly very interested in a vehicle they may have ignored before they entered the hospital.

That is what context does. It takes an idea and places it in the exact moment you need it. And it's so powerful that it can even turn an ad into content.

For instance, when I worked at AutoTrader.com, a fantastic company, our most popular page was our search feature. When someone would search for a car, we would show them an ad. If you were looking for a used Honda Civic and we showed you a promotion for a home mortgage, that was an ad. That was out of context.

If, however, you were looking for a new car because you were moving to a new house and were going to have a longer commute, that same promotion would no longer be an ad. It would be content, something helpful we provided you at the moment you needed it.

To jump back to our store metaphor, context is what you put by the registers. Target doesn't stock televisions by the register because they'd be out of context. No one while checking out has ever said, "Oh, good, I meant to pick up a 42-inch television, and there's one right here by the register!" Instead, Target puts small items there: batteries, ChapStick, things you forgot to get in the store but are likely to buy at the last minute. They put their products (content) in the right place (context).

Where will you share your content?

Where are people looking for your content?

Are they in a season of life in which your content would help them?

## 10. Start slow and small.

The guy who created *Pocket-Sized Stories* isn't writing anymore, which is a shame, because his site was great. What happened? I'm not sure, but he may have fallen prey to the problem that wrecks a lot of people online. Production. The hardest part of social media is keeping the content going. Lots of people start with goals that are too ambitious. They say, "I'll blog every day!" Then by week three, after twenty-one posts, they're exhausted and give up. Pace your social media the right way by starting slow. If you blog, commit to two posts a week for three months. That's only twenty-four posts in ninety days, which is very doable. And it's always better to add content for your readers than it is to take it away. Readers love when you say, "I've been blogging two days a week, but have loved doing it, so I'm going to increase it to three days a week." They get frustrated when you say, "I've been blogging six days a week but can't do it anymore and have to cut back to two days a week."

Don't set out to conquer the world one tweet at a time only to quit on day three when you realize it's a really big world.

# APPENDIX B

# 10 THINGS TO DO IF YOU'RE UNEMPLOYED

**I LOST MY JOB** about an hour after I got married.

This is an exaggeration, but it does reflect what my in-laws probably thought about the whole situation.

I moved their Georgian daughter to Boston for my job after our wedding and then promptly lost it. Those were not fun months.

And a lot of people are in the same place right now. Whether you lost your job or graduated from college into an economy that doesn't feel friendly, there are ten things you need to do right now.

## 1. Remind yourself what you lost.

You didn't lose your identity; you lost your job. Fear and doubt always try to flip that around, to make you think you lost who you are when you lost a job or didn't get one right out of college. Nonsense. You didn't lose your identity; you lost a job title. You lost a seat in a building. You can still be a great dad, a great wife, a great friend, and a million other people right now. Don't listen to fear and doubt in this moment.

## 2. Be honest about the calendar.

The second lie fear will tell you in this moment is that this is forever. It's not a week or a month or even a year you'll be out of work; this is the rest of your life. You will never find another job again. Nobody hires 50-year-olds or 20-year-olds. You will be unemployed for the next three decades. Not true. This is a season, and though it always feels longer than we want, it will come to a conclusion. I promise.

## 3. Flip the numbers.

I honestly believe this is the best time in the history of mankind to find a new job. Twenty years ago you couldn't go online and research entire industries in a matter of minutes. You couldn't apply to 100 jobs in a single day or find quick-hit freelance gigs on Craigslist. But when you watch the news and follow the national unemployment rate like a stock price. it can get discouraging. So next time you hear the unemployment numbers, I want you to flip them. A 22-year-old college senior taught me this. I told him I'd heard the unemployment rate was high for college graduates. He smiled and told me, "Sure, the unemployment rate is high. But even if it's 20 percent, that just means you have to be in the top 80 percent. You can't be a B-minus?" Flip the numbers.

## 4. Think about your circles.

Being unemployed is about properly managing three different circles: Geography, Industry, and Commitment. The longer you are unemployed, the more deliberate you have to be about expanding these circles. For example, in the first month or two you may just look for a new job in your city. During the second and third months, you may expand your search to other cities in your state. If you experience prolonged unemployment, you may need to expand your search to other states, even other time zones. Same goes with the industry you search in and the commitment you want (full-time, part-time, or hourly). Want to potentially speed up your job search? Expand the circles quickly.

## 5. Finding a job is your new job.

Don't ever think of yourself as jobless. The minute you get laid off or graduate without a job lined up, you get a new job. It's called "finding a job." That is your forty-hour-a-week, full-time job. Enlist a friend who will hold you accountable and help you track the results of your "work." Come up with job performance metrics like "resumes sent," "jobs applied for," etc. I don't have hard numbers on how many people actually put in this level of effort to find a new job, but survey the friends you know who are unemployed. Chances are, approximately zero are treating finding a new job as their job.

## 6. Get a stopgap job.

This is 100 percent easier to write in a book than it is to actually do, but that doesn't mean it's not true. You may need to get a stopgap job, some sort of part-time employment that heads off monsters like "getting the power turned off," "having your car repo'd," or "moving back in with your parents." This is an ego-aside, I-never-thought-I'd-work-here-but-difficult-times-call-for-difficult-measures kind of job. For instance, the day I wrote this section of the book, I saw a bakery hiring someone to bake bread from 11:00 p.m. to 7:00 a.m. That's not easy. That's not fun. But that's a great stopgap job. And don't for a second buy the lie, "If I take on a part-time job, I won't be able to go out for interviews or look for a full-time job." That's ridiculous. What job interview are you forced to cancel at 4:00 a.m. because you're making bread?

## 7. Stay in job shape.

Having a job is like running a marathon. And the first thing most people do when they lose theirs is get as fat as possible. We stop getting up early. We give up our schedules. We terminate any sense of structure in our lives and then we occasionally sprint for a job interview, completely confused that we didn't nail it. When you don't have a job, you have to stay in job shape. That was one of my wife's few requirements when I lost my job. She had to be up at 6:30 a.m. for her job, and so did I. So every weekday morning I was showered and dressed, ready for the day to begin. Otherwise, I would have stayed up the night before watching reruns of *Seinfeld* and eating queso in bulk, then sleeping in. Don't get out of job shape just because you don't have a job.

## 8. Get plugged into a community.

As we discussed earlier in this book, fear fears community. Fear always tries to isolate you and put you on an island. That will happen when you lose your job. As fast as you can, and as much as it fits the way you like to engage with people, try to get plugged into a community of people who are looking for new jobs. The economy has created thousands of these. You could go to a community center, a church, your library, or online to find a group that will encourage, challenge, and help you during your season of job searching. Don't go it alone.

## 9. Start a blog.

Or an Instagram feed or Twitter account or Facebook page or whatever technology is hot at the time you're reading this book. Why? Because every job seeker is going to tell the interviewer, "I'm passionate about this industry!" Then the interviewer is going to say, "Really, how so?" Then the job seeker is going to say, "Ways, a lot of different ways. There are so many I can barely just pick one." But you? You're going to say, "Well, I have a blog where I write about the industry. I'm also plugged into the online communities of industry experts. You may like to follow my Twitter account, where I curate the top articles about this industry." You've got tools right now to impress an interviewer that no one ever had before. Use them.

## 10. Put results at the top.

This one is incredibly tactical, but it works. At the top of resumes, most people put "goals" or "objectives." They then type out paragraphs that say things like, "I want to work in a people-based environment where I can use my skills to progress the business in innovative ways." Goals at the top of resumes are useless. Why? Everyone can say the exact same things. Everyone on the planet can write fluffy words about what they're going to do. That doesn't separate you from the crowd.

One time the owner of one of the best ad agencies in the country chewed me out for using empty words like *goals* when I applied at his company. He said that every candidate he interviewed told him over and over again how creative or goal-oriented they were. He didn't care about that. He cared about what I'd actually accomplished.

I rewrote my resume that week. Instead of goals or objectives, I started each resume with a short paragraph titled "Results." In less than 100 words, I summarized what I felt I had accomplished that may be relevant to a certain job.

And something weird happened. Recruiters and HR departments started asking me about the results. In some cases, they barely looked at the rest of my resume and would just say, "What was it like to work at Home Depot?" No one had ever asked me about any of the meaningless sentences I had put in my "goals" paragraph.

Maybe it will be easy to write your accomplishments or results paragraph. But even if it's not, I promise that you've done something interesting and important in your career. If you worked at a job for a year or two, I'm just talking about creating one interesting sentence from that whole experience. One year of work, one sentence. Anyone—and I repeat, anyone—can do that.

Even if you're a recent college grad just joining a new industry, you've got a sentence or two you could put in that paragraph that may generate questions, interest, and maybe even a job interview. You've got four years of college from which to pull a few sentences.

The good news is that regardless of why you find yourself without a job, there are some very tactical things you can do to remedy that. The great news is that we're all 20. We all have the chance to start over and be awesome again.

Just because you're unemployed doesn't mean you have to be average.

# NOTES

## Chapter 1

1. Glenn Ruffenach, "Eyeing an Encore Career? Expect a Bumpy Transition," *Smart Money*, July 2, 2012, http://www .smartmoney.com/retirement/planning/eyeing-an-encore -career-expect-a-bumpy-transition-1339526090060/.

2. Boris Cerni and Zachary Tracer, "AIG Chief Sees Retirement Age as High as 80 after Crisis," Bloomberg, June 4, 2012, http://www.bloomberg.com/news/2012-06-03/aig-chief -sees-retirement-age-as-high-as-80-after-crisis.html.

3. "Pebble: E-Paper Watch for iPhone and Android," Pebble Technology, http://www.kickstarter.com/projects/597507018 /pebble-e-paper-watch-for-iphone-and-android.

## Chapter 2

1. Adam Horowitz and the editors of *Business 2.0, The Dumbest Moments in Business History: Useless Products, Ruinous Deals, Clueless Bosses and Other Signs of Unintelligent Life in the Workplace*, comps. Mark Athitakis and Mark Lasswell (New York: Portfolio, 2004), 146.

2. Kathryn Stockett, "Kathryn Stockett's 'The Help' Turned Down 60 Times Before Becoming a Best Seller," *More*, May 7, 2011, http://www.more.com/kathryn-stockett-help -best-seller.

3. Jim Collins, *Good to Great: Why Some Companies Make the Leap . . . and Others Don't* (New York: HarperCollins, 2001), 85.

4. John Mayer, "Walt Grace's Submarine Test, January 1967," on *Born and Raised*, Columbia, 2012, CD.

## Chapter 3

1. Stephen R. Covey, "Habit 2: Begin With the End in Mind," *The 7 Habits of Highly Effective People*, https://www.stephen covey.com/7habits/7habits-habit2.php.

2. Malcolm Gladwell, *Outliers: The Story of Success* (New York: Little, Brown and Company, 2008), 38.

3. Matthew Syed, *Bounce: Mozart, Federer, Picasso, Beckham, and the Science of Success* (New York: Harper Collins, 2010), 57.

4. Deirdre Donahue, "Malcolm Gladwell's 'Success' Defines 'Outlier' Achievement," *USA Today*, November 18, 2008, http://usatoday30.usatoday.com/life/books/news/2008-11 -17-gladwell-success_N.htm.

5. Grant Oyston, "Success?" *Visible Children* (blog), March 9, 2012, http://visiblechildren.tumblr.com/post/18992455677 /success.

6. Grant Oyston, "What was my intent?" *Visible Children* (blog), March 7, 2012, http://visiblechildren.tumblr.com /post/18917304254/what-was-my-intent.

7. Ramona Emerson, "Comedians on Technology: Louis C.K., Mitch Hedberg, Bill Murray and Others Rant About Tech," *Huffington Post*, February 20, 2012, http: //www.huffingtonpost.com/2012/02/20/comedians-on -technology_n_1108931.html.

8. Steven Pressfield, *The War of Art: Break Through the Blocks and Win Your Inner Creative Battles* (New York: Black Irish Entertainment LLC, 2002), 12.

## Chapter 4

1. Charles Duhigg, *The Power of Habit: Why We Do What We Do in Life and Business* (New York: Random House, 2012), 135–37.

2. Tony Schwartz, Jean Gomes, and Catherine McCarthy, *The Way We're Working Isn't Working: The Four Forgotten Needs That Energize Great Performance* (New York: Free Press, 2010), 33–35.

3. Susie Steiner, "Top Five Regrets of the Dying," *The Guardian*, February 1, 2012, http://www.guardian.co.uk/lifeandstyle /2012/feb/01/top-five-regrets-of-the-dying.

4. Josh Linkner, "The Dirty Little Secret of Overnight Successes," *Fast Company*, April 2, 2012, http://www.fastcompany.com /1826976/the-dirty-little-secret-of-overnight-successes.

## Chapter 5

1. Robert T. Gonzalez, "Ten gemstones that are rarer than diamond," io9, April 16, 2012, http://io9.com/5902212 /ten-gemstones-that-are-rarer-than-diamond.

2. Gene Weingarten, "Pearls Before Breakfast," *Washington Post*, April 8, 2007, http://www.washingtonpost.com /wp-dyn/content/article/2007/04/04/AR2007040401721 .html.

3. Ori Brafman and Rom Brafman, *Sway: The Irresistible Pull of Irrational Behavior*, (New York: Doubleday, 2008), 50.

4. Bill Watterson, *The Calvin and Hobbes Tenth Anniversary Book*, (Kansas City: Universal Press Syndicate, 1995), 11.

## Chapter 6

1. Twyla Tharp with Mark Reiter, *The Creative Habit: Learn It and Use It for Life* (New York: Simon & Schuster, 2005), 9.
2. Brian Hiatt, "The Neurotic Zen of Larry David," *Rolling Stone*, August 4, 2011, 81.
3. Kevin Freiberg and Jackie Freiberg, *NUTS! Southwest Airlines' Crazy Recipe for Business and Personal Success* (New York: Broadway Books, 1997), 269–70.

## Chapter 7

1. Nancy Hass, "Love Me, Hate Me, Just Don't Ignore Me," *GQ*, February 2012, 52.
2. Andy Warhol, *The Stockholm Catalog*, Pontus Hulten, Kasper Konig, and Olle Granath, eds. (Stockholm: Moderna Museet, 1968).
3. John shared this idea at North Point Community Church. He shares more brilliant ideas on his blog, www.jdubspubs.com.
4. Sydney Lupkin, "Can Facebook Ruin Your Marriage?" ABC News, May 24, 2012, http://abcnews.go.com/Technology /facebook-relationship-status/story?id=16406245 #.UClhiZi4LzI.
5. Anne B. Fisher, "Are You Afraid of Success?" *Fortune*, July 8, 1996, http://money.cnn.com/magazines/fortune/fortune _archive/1996/07/08/214330/.
6. Buck Brannaman, *Buck*. Directed by Cindy Meehl (IFC Films, 2011).

## Chapter 8

1. Derek Sivers, "Obvious to you. Amazing to others," (YouTube video) April 19, 2011, http://www.youtube.com/watch?v=-GCm-u_vlaQ&feature=player_embedded.

2. Jim Collins, "Good to Great and the Social Sectors: Why Business Thinking Is Not the Answer" (excerpt), November 2005, http://www.jimcollins.com/books/g2g-ss.html.

3. Andy Bull, "David Rudisha breaks world record to win Olympic 800m gold for Kenya," *Guardian*, August 9, 2012, http://www.guardian.co.uk/sport/2012/aug/09/david-rudisha-world-record-olympic-800m?newsfeed=true.

4. Mike Rosenbaum, "800 Meter Men's Olympic Medalists," About.com Track & Field, http://trackandfield.about.com/od/middledistance/qt/olym800men.htm.

5. Andy Bull, "David Rudisha breaks world record to win Olympic 800m gold for Kenya," *Guardian*, August 9, 2012, http://www.guardian.co.uk/sport/2012/aug/09/david-rudisha-world-record-olympic-800m?newsfeed=true.

6. Steven Pressfield, *The War of Art: Break Through the Blocks and Win Your Inner Creative Battles* (New York: Black Irish Entertainment LLC, 2002), 166.

7. Erick Calonius, *Ten Steps Ahead: What Separates Successful Business Visionaries from the Rest of Us* (New York: Penguin, 2011), 194–95.

## Appendix A

1. Amir Efrati, "The Mounting Minuses at Google+," *Wall Street Journal*, February 28, 2012, http://online.wsj.com/article/SB10001424052970204653604577249341403742390.html.

2. *Pocket-Sized Stories* (blog), http://pocketsizedstories.tumblr
.com/.

# ACKNOWLEDGMENTS

First and foremost, God. Thank you for being the God who fixes problems with parties, who welcomes prodigals with open arms.

Jenny Acuff, my ridiculously awesome wife. Without you I'd be in a gutter somewhere writing Goth poetry. I love you, L.E. and McRae. I can't wait to read the books you write someday! Mom and Dad, thanks for teaching me to dream. Will, Tiffany, Bennett, Sally, Mac, Sawyer, and Molly Acuff. John and Laura Calbert, the best in-laws a guy could have. Marci and Justin Saknini.

Dave Ramsey, who is constantly daring me to start. Your support of this project has been nothing short of amazing. Preston Cannon for believing in this book when it was just an idea on a napkin. Jeremy Breland for fighting for this project alongside me. Jen Sievertsen, Katie Crenshaw, Brian Williams, Luke LeFevre, Erin McAtee, Darcie Clemen (who made this book so much better!), Neal Webb, Liz Edwards, Beth Tallent, Chris Mefford (my favorite Canadian), Steve NeSmith, Josh Holloway, Lisa Mays, Dawn Medley (you are awesome!) and the entire team at Dave Ramsey for their unbelievable help.

Brent Cole, best editor on the planet. Mrs. Harris, Grant Jenkins, Stephen Brewster, Mike Foster, Al Andrews (who was quoted a billion times!), Bob Goff, Mike, Lynn, Wendy, and Erin Maybury. Steven Pressfield. And all the readers of my blogs. I don't get to write books without your generosity.

Thank you.

# CONTINUE THE CONVERSATION

## BLOG

jonacuff.com

## TWITTER

@jonacuff

## FACEBOOK

facebook.com/authorjonacuff

## PINTEREST

pinterest.com/jonacuff

## INSTAGRAM

jonacuff

## SHARE YOUR VOICES

nomorevoices.com

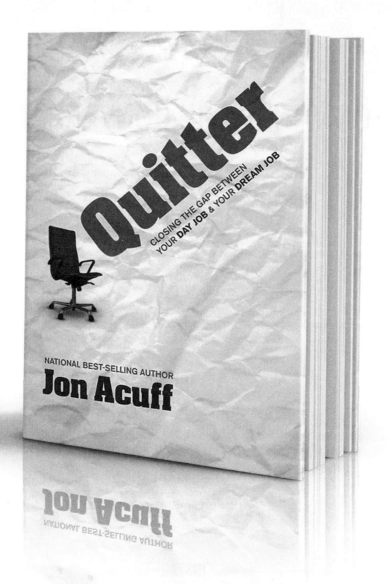

**CLOSE THE GAP BETWEEN YOUR DAY JOB AND YOUR DREAM JOB.**

Available at bookstores everywhere
or at **daveramsey.com/store**